Rebel In White

Bertha McConish

Rebel In White

Bertha McComish

With Maggie Martin

ISBN:1492387363
ISBN:9781492387367

For nurses, past, present and future
and
for my sister, Mary
my son, Tim, and his children, Kelsey, Megan, Cathy, and Timmy
my son, Dennis, and his son, Joshua
and for my daughter, Nancy, and her children, Sophie and Abby

CONTENTS

FOREWORD

When Bertha McComish asked me to contribute a foreword to the account she had compiled of her career in nursing, she had no way of knowing how familiar I was with the life and work of a nurse.

Since the age of eight or nine until I was a teenager, I had looked forward to the monthly visits of my Aunt Imogene, my Mother's younger sister.

We lived in Easton, Pennsylvania, about an hour from Jersey City, New Jersey, where Imogene worked at the very large Jersey City Medical Center, a complex of hospitals. Her nursing units were in the TB hospital, where she oversaw care of all its male patients with very little help, as World War II was then in full force, causing a severe nursing shortage here in the U.S. One of her TB wards became particularly difficult for Imogene, as she had fallen in love with one of her patients. She was thrilled when he presented her with an engagement ring, but it was a bittersweet experience, for he soon died.

Nursing requires not only the specialized knowledge care of the sick demands, but also an empathy for and an understanding of the human condition. All are present in this compelling memoir of an expert nurse and a warm human being.

Jill C. Wilson

Hopkinton, NH

CHAPTER ONE
FROM DRIVING OXEN TO DRINKING TEA

On September 4, 1945, my mother parked our Model A Ford directly in front of the Nurses' Residence for Memorial Hospital, at 60 South Street in Concord, New Hampshire, and I had my first sight of my new home for the next three years. The front door opened into a hallway, with an entrance to the living room on my left. Suitcase and laundry bag in hand, I walked right into that room, looked around, and saw my future classmates. And I saw Ladies, Ladies, Ladies! Mothers of students, doctors' wives and hospital trustees, all of the Ladies were wearing fancy hats and gloves, and with pinky fingers extended, holding china tea cups. I had blundered into a Welcoming Tea for in-coming students, with no clue as to what I should do.

I had been asked to deliver a bottle of nail polish to a friend and fellow classmate. "Your mother sent this with me, because you forgot it!" I blurted out when I saw her, my voice too loud for the tea party atmosphere. I realized in that moment, that I had much to learn in this new place and time in my life, but I also felt confident that I could. I had spent my early years on our family's farm on Craney Hill in Henniker, a small town in southern New Hampshire. With no neighbors close by, no children from other families to play with, the only time my younger sister, Mary and I saw friends was at school. I may not have learned how to act properly at a tea party, but I had learned the value of hard work on the farm, and I knew how to do it well. When my dad gave me a job to do, he assumed I was able to do

1

it. One of the first times I can remember Dad's faith in me goes back to the day my brother, Forrest, was born. It was the summer of 1937. I was ten, and Mary was eight.

In those days, Henniker women had the choice of going to the town's Maternity Home to birth their children, rather than have a mid-wife or doctor come to their farms or homes to assist. When it was close to her time, Dad drove Mother to the Maternity Home on Hall Avenue; Mary and I went along. When we arrived, we discovered that nobody was at home. Mother told Dad to take us back to the big house on Craney Hill, where she called the doctor and told him to come out to the summer cottage Dad had built for visiting relatives and friends from the city who enjoyed spending time in the country. To get there from our house, you went down the hill, past the sheds to the fork in the dirt road, took the right fork to the unpaved road that came up to Craney Hill from town, and crossed it. Right there in the field stood the cottage, clean and unoccupied, a perfect place to have the baby. This time, Mary and I stayed behind in the big house, alone and scared.

It was supper time, and still no baby, when Dad came back and told me to fix something for the doctor to eat, leaving it up to me to think of what to prepare. But before I could cook anything, I had to start the kitchen wood stove. I put in the dry, pine kindling, doused it with kerosene, and lit it with a wooden match. Then I added hardwood. While I waited for the fire to heat up the oven, I made baking powder biscuits from scratch. We didn't have a refrigerator or electricity, so I got the milk and butter from where we kept them, in a pail lowered far enough into the well to keep them cold, but not wet. After I put the biscuits in the oven, I got the kerosene lantern and made my way down the steep steps to the dark, cool cellar to get the great piece of bacon that hung there. I carried it up, and with the sharp kitchen knife Mother had taught me to use, cut off strips to fry.

From the cellar shelves, where she stored her canned goods, I got a quart jar of Mother's preserved string beans. My parents didn't drink tea or coffee, so when Dad came to get the doctor's meal, he gave him some cold, clear water from the cottage well.

Dad finally returned to the house that night and told Mary and me that we had a brother. He also explained that his mother would be staying at the cottage to help with the new baby. When my sister and I went to see Forrest for the first time, Mother told me, "Bertha, Grammie doesn't have the stomach to empty my bed pan; you will have to do it." I didn't fuss. I just took it to the outhouse and emptied it.

Back then, it was customary for women to stay in bed for a week or more after giving birth, but Mother was only two or three days into her confinement when Grammie was cooking breakfast and the bacon in the frying pan caught on fire. Hearing her mother-in-law yell, "Fire!" Mother jumped out of bed and doused the flames with baking soda. I guess she decided that since she was up, she might as well stay up. Mother and Forrest moved back to the big house, and Grammie Morse went home.

The following winter brought an outbreak of Influenza. By then I was eleven, and Mary was nine. Our parents must have been terribly sick to not be able to get out of bed and take care of the farm animals. A pair of oxen, a horse, six heifers, and the milking cow needed to be let out of their places in the barn, watered and fed, then tied up again where they belonged, and my sister and I were being told that it was up to us.

It was scary seeing Dad in bed, too weak to do anything, and it was scary thinking about going to the barn without him. I had watched, and even helped him with these late afternoon and early evening chores, but I had never done them alone. Knowing that he depended on us, Mary and I pulled ourselves out of the warmth and security of the house and made our way to the barn.

First to go for water were the oxen. They were nearest to the steps my father had built for the animals to go down under the barn and out to the lane that led to the spring, each step the width of three logs. I carried an axe as Mary and I went along. Patiently, the oxen waited at the spring, while I stood legs apart so as not to cut off my feet, and chopped away at the ice to make a hole big enough for them to drink.

When they'd had their fill, we drove the oxen back along the lane, into the barn, and secured them. Next, the cattle. Mary and I let the cow out first, followed by the six heifers. We made sure they didn't crowd into one spot at the watering hole, and after they'd all had their turn, we followed them back to the barn.

Now, the cow had been trained and knew her place, but the heifers behaved more like adolescents. They didn't care where they went, so some of them didn't return to their own stalls. With Mary on one side and me on the other, each of us using a stick, we would back one critter out of the wrong stall and head her into the right one. But another heifer might be in it, so we'd have to back that one out and head her into her own stall, already occupied by the wrong heifer. All of this backing-out and heading-in was causing confusion that could be repeated many times. Well, my eleven year old self took control of the mix-up, and in the end, each animal was in her right place. I was glad of Mary's help.

The horse, his heels clattering on the wooden stairs, was the last to go for water. We were relieved when he finished drinking, because it was getting dark. The milking cow still had to be milked, and all of the animals, including the pigs, hens, and sheep, had to be fed. Mary and I went back to the house to get the kerosene lantern, so that we'd have some light, while we fed them.

With great care, I hung the lantern on the hook at the end of the rope that went around the windlass, a big wooden wheel secured in the upper part of the barn. Dad used the windlass to pull up a butchered hog within our reach, so we could easily remove its bristles and all of its internal organs. Even though I knew that the rope was securely fastened, I was still afraid that if I let go and the lantern fell onto the hay on the barn floor, it would surely set the barn on fire. I

4

had to make a decision. I let go of the rope and was relieved to see the lantern still hanging in mid-air, its faint light casting shadows in the hay mow.

Mary steadied the wooden ladder, while I climbed up to get the hay to feed the animals. I wasn't afraid, until I was about to step off the top rung and realized I might slip on the scatterings of dry hay on the mow's edge and fall, but I made it safely and pitched the loose hay from the back of the mow onto the barn floor. After I climbed back down, we used our hayforks to push the hay in front of each of the animals inside the barn waiting to be fed. They were hungry!

Once the indoor animals were fed, Mary and I went back to the house to get the potato peelings, scraps of table food, and the water that had been saved during the day, so we could mix them with grain to feed the pigs who lived in a pen under the barn. When the slop was ready, we poured it into the chute that went down to their trough.

I don't remember much of what happened, after Mary and I finished. It had been a long night. I do remember that within days, the story of what she and I had done made its way off Craney Hill and into the town newspaper. The headline read: *Had a Test Beyond Testing.*

As we got older, among the chores Mary and I were able to help with was tending the galvanized buckets that collected sap from the maple trees in the orchard, near Craney Pond when it was time for Dad to make maple syrup. He would hand-drill holes, about the size of a man's middle finger, into the trees and insert hooked, metal spouts deep enough for the sap to run down and into the open-top, two-gallon buckets my sister and I had hung on the hooks. When the buckets needed emptying, she and I would go around the orchard and empty them into pails, and then carry the sap to the gathering tank and pour it in. Those pails were heavy! If it rained, however, we would have to empty the buckets onto the ground, because it would cost more to boil the diluted sap than it was worth.

It was my responsibility to haul the tank of sap on an oxen-driven scoot to the sap house, where Dad boiled it down into syrup. I had to take extra care so that the scoot didn't get hung up on the rocks that surfaced after the deep snow had melted. I knew that if the tank tipped over, it would mean a physical hardship for my father, because he would have to leave the sap house and come to the orchard. It would also cause a financial hardship. Selling maple syrup was one of the ways Dad made money to buy what we didn't provide for ourselves on the farm. I had to make sure that tank of sap never tipped over. It never did.

If Dad had something in mind for Mary and me to do, his way was to tell Mother, and then Mother would tell us. One day, she informed us that Dad wanted us to get the oxen and dump cart and go to the field to bring back a pile of wood. I had already helped him when he was sawing the four-foot logs into stove-length pieces; my job had been to "take away." Standing with my feet apart to keep from losing my balance and falling into the unprotected blade, I had held each piece of wood, as Dad sawed it with the three-foot circular saw. When it was free, I tossed it onto a pile behind me.

I complained to Mother, probably for the first time, when I heard what I was expected to do. "The kids in town don't have to work like I have to!" She was quiet for a moment, before gently responding, "Someday you'll be glad you did." My teen-aged reply: "That will be the day!"

Dad assigned our chores, but he had also told us early on, "Don't stand around waiting for someone to tell you what to do. Look around, see what needs to be done, and do it." I had taken his words to heart when I was around eleven and had gone with my family to visit our neighbors, about a mile down the road from our farm.

The husband, who probably had Phlebitis, had been confined to a sitting position, with his leg elevated on the hassock. As the grown-ups talked, I learned that he was alone all day while his wife worked, so I decided that I would go and read to him. My parents didn't object when I told them my plan. The next day, I walked the mile to his house by myself, and while I read to him, I pretended that I was his nurse.

During the summer of my thirteenth year, I worked as a live-in helper for another neighbor and her family. I had been around six or seven when she got married, and I had joined my family in a custom from my part of New England called, *Horning*. Friends and neighbors from surrounding farms went to a newly-wed couple's house on their wedding night, waited until the lights were out, and then woke them by shaking cow bells and banging on pots and pans. When they got out of bed, they were expected to serve refreshments to everyone!
I remember eating strawberries that night.

By the time I entered my teens, our neighbor and her husband had two young children. I understood that she needed help, but no one gave me an explanation for why she was having difficulty walking. I cooked and cleaned for her and her family, without knowing that she had Multiple Sclerosis, but I did know, instinctively, to rub her legs. I told her that I was going to be a nurse some day, and that I would come back and take care of her.

On Sunday afternoons during that summer, I walked the three miles from my house to my neighbors'. Entering my father's field, to the right of the summer cottage, I'd make my way through the rows of summer corn for about two hundred feet, until I came to a stone wall. On the other side of the wall, I'd set out on the trail through the woods that led to Mount Hunger. I'm sure there must have been a time when Dad had shown us landmarks, but now I looked for my own, paying attention to the rocks and trees along the twists and turns. Almost at the end of the trail stood a big spruce tree, where I'd stop and dig out a clump of dried spruce juice from the bark and chew it. The taste was tart. I didn't like it all that much, but it was the closest thing we had to chewing gum, and anything was better than nothing.

7

Beyond the spruce tree, I came to a little knoll, and as I walked down, I knew I would soon step out of the woods and onto the lawn of the McComish homestead. If Mr. McComish happened to be out working, he'd greet me, and I'd stop for a chat, before continuing onto Mount Hunger Road, a dirt road, like all the roads on all the hills in Henniker. I'd only have a short distance to walk, before turning left and up the hill to my neighbors' homestead. On Friday, in the late afternoon, I retraced my steps to Craney Hill. Since it was assumed that I would get to where I was going, nobody ever checked to see if I'd arrived at my destination in either direction.

I approached the neighbors' house one Sunday and saw that their black and white Collie was loose. He was a good cow dog, but he was also a good protector when the family was away. I knew he was not going to let me walk up to the front door and go inside. I was scared at first, but when I realized that he hadn't seen me yet, I went back down the hill, climbed over the stone wall that ran along the cow pasture, snuck around to the back of the house, and entered through the unlocked door. The family was surprised to find me when they returned, but I knew I had work inside that I was responsible for.

I had been brought up to find a way to do what needed doing, and not get stopped by obstacles. However, a few years later, there would be one obstacle that neither I nor my family could overcome, and it would change our lives in a way that none of us ever expected.

The sixty-plus acres of land that my father farmed and took care of on Craney Hill belonged to his uncle, who lived in town. Uncle Wallace had promised that in exchange for working the farm, Dad would inherit all of the land and the buildings on it. I was a junior in high school when Uncle Wallace had a stroke, or at least that's what I've come to believe. His wife, my Great Aunt Ida, was probably not able to take care of him on her own, and since there were no nursing homes at the time, a woman from town became Uncle Wallace's care-taker. She took over his life, refusing to allow any of his family to see him. Apparently, Aunt Ida was powerless to do to anything about it.

After Uncle Wallace died, all of his properties in town and all of the acreage and buildings on Craney Hill belonged to that woman. A letter was sent to my father ordering us off the hill. I don't know if any lawyers were involved, but I do know that Dad didn't fight the eviction. That wasn't his way. We would leave Craney Hill. But where would we go?

I came home from school one day and told my parents that I'd seen a house for sale, about a mile from town, on Gulf Road. Dad looked at the property and found it agreeable. There were fields to plant and a barn for the animals.

As sad as I was to leave Craney Hill, I also felt an excitement about moving. I could walk to town. I could be more like the kids who lived there. I no longer had to miss out on social activities with friends. Mother wouldn't have to drive us to school and pick us up, which she could only do as long as the roads were open. In the winter, there was so much snow that, even though the roads had been plowed, it was impossible to use a car to get off, or get back up Craney Hill. Dad relied on the oxen and horse and cart to go for necessary supplies, like grain to feed the animals. In spring, mud was the culprit.

During the worst of the winter, for most of our childhood, Mother would give up being with Dad from Monday to Friday, to stay with Mary and me in Uncle Wallace's workshop, close to his house in town, so we could go to school. The unheated shed had no electricity or water, and was divided into two small rooms, beyond Uncle's workspace. Mother, Mary, and I slept in the same bed in one of the rooms. No indoor plumbing meant no bathroom, only a chemical toilet, which Mother emptied, daily. There was a three burner, kerosene stove in the other, partitioned-off room, where Mother cooked our meals.

I have often wondered, as an adult, why Uncle Wallace never put us up in his house. Sometimes I think it might have been because he and Aunt Ida had married late in life, were set in their ways, and didn't want children interfering with their routine. But I don't remember Mother being invited to spend time in the house with them, either. Maybe she did visit while we were at school. I'll never really know what arrangements the grown-ups had made, but I do know that the quilt Aunt Ida had made for Mary and me kept us warm, and that we had fun running around inside the shed, in spite of Mother's concern that we'd knock over the kerosene stove. The most fun was shoe-skating on the frozen water in the gully near the road, in front of Uncle Wallace's house, with Mary and the boy next door.

In March of 1943, I was nearly sixteen when Mother gave birth to my sister, Lois, in the Henniker Maternity Home. A month later, we all moved to Gulf Road, where Dad began the work of making the house and the land his own. Our family settled in, and I continued my routine of school and work, but not like on Craney Hill. Dad was working at a local poultry farm, so after school and on weekends, I painted hen houses and graded eggs, for pay! I got thirty-five cents an hour to paint two-story hen houses an old-fashioned red. I can't remember how much I got for grading the eggs.

Toward the end of my senior year of high school, I took an aptitude test, which confirmed that I was suited for a career in nursing. With the school principal's encouragement, I submitted my application to train to be a nurse through the Federal Government's Cadet Nurse Corps, which had been instituted to address the shortage of nurses created by World War II. Run by the. U. S. Public Health Service's Division of Nurse Education, the Corps provided prospective nurses with a free education and a monthly stipend. It also issued uniforms and berets for the cadets to wear, in addition to their home hospital uniforms.

Two hospitals in Concord, New Hampshire became units of the Corps, the Margaret Pillsbury Hospital in 1943, followed by the Memorial Hospital in 1944. I was happy to learn that I had been accepted into the Memorial Hospital's unit.

Like many young women of my era, I would not have been able to study nursing without the Cadet Nurse Corps, and like my fellow members, I was committed to serve my country after graduation, when and where needed. The war ended before I graduated, freeing me from the commitment to serve.

CHAPTER TWO
AFTER THE TEA PARTY: WORK!

The distance from Henniker to Concord is twenty-three miles, a long way at a time when cars didn't travel more than twenty-five miles an hour. If they went forty miles an hour, they were going too fast! My family had to have a good reason to make a trip that went so far and took up so much time; perhaps Dad needed an inner tube for a tire, or Mother, a ration of sugar for canning. But now, I was going to live in Concord and study to become a nurse.

Having experienced how it felt to be uprooted from our home on Craney Hill, moving to the city didn't seem as difficult as it might have been. Memorial Hospital's policy of assigning Big Sisters to new-comers also helped ease the transition. These upper-class students helped us get acquainted with our new residence and the city, as well.

I met my Big Sister for the first time at the Welcoming Tea. She addressed me as "Miss Morse" when she took my suitcase and showed me to my room—third floor, second room down the hall, on the right. On our way, she reminded me of some of the more important house rules, from among the five pages of rules and regulations the hospital had enclosed with my acceptance.

As a beginning student, I was not allowed to socialize with upper-class students, except at school functions. No resident was permitted to draw a bath between 9:45 p.m., and 10:00 a.m., so as not to disturb nurses who were sleeping after a shift. All students, regardless of rank, were forbidden to be married or to get married during their preparation for a career in nursing. At the time, my Big Sister and I had no way of knowing that she would break that rule. The fact that she didn't get pregnant made it easier to keep her marriage a secret, and for her to graduate without getting caught. By that time, I was no longer known as Miss Morse. I had become "Morsie." Of course, nicknames were only used when we were off-duty.

Room assignments in the residence were made according to the students' entrance date into the three-year study of Theory and Practice. There were fourteen of us in my Freshman Class sharing rooms on the third floor, two in each room. One room had three. We also shared the two baths, each with a tub, sink, and toilet.

An indoor bathroom with hot, running water was a luxury for me. On Craney Hill, we carted water from the well house and heated it on the wood stove. To get to the out-house, we went through the kitchen, into the summer kitchen, then into the attached shed, where Dad kept his tools on a long, wood bench. Beyond it was the door to the attached two-holer, about four feet wide. I guess you could say that since the house and the shed were attached, we never really went outside to get to the outhouse

Living a self-sufficient life meant that we made and grew what we needed, with a few exceptions, and put everything we had to good use, so for toilet paper, we crumpled up old mail-order catalogues to make them soft. Since I had never considered using the outhouse a hardship, I certainly didn't have a problem sharing an indoor bathroom in the nurses' residence, not even when some of us had to brush our teeth at the tub faucet because of a crowd around the sink, as we got ready for morning inspection.

Students going on duty in the hospital at 6:55 a.m. assembled for inspection at 6:30 a.m. in the residence living room. We stood in rows, according to seniority. I remember stepping aside one morning to make room for a senior weaving her way to her place in the front row, still buttoning the back of her apron.

The night supervisor, or sometimes the nursing superintendent, inspected us from our white caps and required hair nets to our shoes and laces, as we passed her in single file, wearing our stiffly starched, white, cotton aprons over our blue and white soft, cotton dresses, fitted with stiff, detachable collars and cuffs. Our hair nets and caps: Perfect! Shoes: Polished! Shoe laces: White! White! White! Morning inspection was also a time of prayer and hymn singing. Our favorite hymn? *Work! For the Night Is Coming.*

We were not allowed back to our rooms after breakfast in the hospital dining room. We were expected to report to work on our assigned floors, and work we did! Six days a week, frequently working a split shift, in addition to attending our classes. We were "In Training." When our supervisors said, "Jump!" we jumped. If a doctor, or others senior to us in rank, walked into the room, we stood up, especially in the hospital's chart room. You can imagine we spent a lot of time getting in and out of our chairs.

On shift, we had a half-hour for meals, which included the walk to and from the dining room. Holding our empty trays, we made our way in a line, through the narrow door to the kitchen, stopping long enough for kitchen staff to put plates of food on them. There was no "Special of the Day" for us; we got what was served, whether we liked it or not.

The dining room had about fifteen tables, all of them covered with linen table cloths and arrayed with place settings of silverware. Senior students and RNs sat at designated tables; underclass students had their own assigned places and were forbidden to join them. In the far right corner of the room, near the window, doctors dined at reserved tables and were waited on by dining room staff. I'll never forget one of the waitresses because of her bright red lipstick.

After the morning's work on our assigned unit, and our mid-day dinner, our afternoons were spent attending classes. We returned to the dining room for supper, and then to our rooms for evening study time. Maintaining this rigorous schedule allowed us to complete four years of training in three, with an annual three week vacation. School and work were all I had known, so I had no trouble adjusting, but I can see where some of my classmates, accustomed to more freedom, would have had a hard time. Although I can't say for certain what their reasons were, two members of my class did drop out in the first few weeks of training.

At the end of our six-month probationary period, if we passed Theory and Practice, we were entitled to add a stiff, white bib and a white cap to our uniform. To honor our accomplishment, the hospital held a Capping Ceremony at a local church. After successfully completing a year of training, we earned the right to add a quarter-inch, black velvet stripe to the cap; after our second year, another quarter-inch, black velvet stripe. Successful completion of the third year, meant we could replace both quarter-inch stripes with a three-quarter inch, black velvet band.

Nurses' uniforms and caps were considered status symbols, with rules for wearing them—dress: fifteen inches from the floor; apron, fourteen and one-half inches. Caps were creased to three inches width, and held in place with the required, three white bobby pins— two in back, and one, center front. The hospital provided laundering and ironing for our uniforms, but not until we had worn them for two consecutive days. We made sure we didn't lean against anything that would soil our starched aprons, and to prevent them from wrinkling when we sat, we learned to separate the panels of fabric in the back, gather them forward, and carefully rest them on our laps.

Unlike our cadet uniforms, we were not allowed to wear our hospital uniforms in public. We were also forbidden to wear them in our residence's recreation room. We were permitted to "lounge" there, in housecoats and lounging pajamas, but only as long as we had "presentably dressed-hair." When we were off-duty, "proper street dress," and make-up were acceptable in class, as were socks with sports clothes, in the hospital dining room, and in our residence.

During study hours, the doors to our rooms remained open. Oh yes, we had to toe the mark. No running or unnecessary talking in the corridors. No radios. No loud talking or laughing at any time. Our house mother monitored our noise levels, making certain to let us know when we were too noisy. Once during study time, we were laughing so loudly, we could be heard on the first floor. The house mother called up to us to be quiet and had begun climbing the stairs, but we were having such a good time, we never heard her. Fortunately, someone saw her on the stairwell and warned us in time. We all scampered to our rooms!

Students weren't the only occupants of the residence. A room on the second floor was home to the superintendent of nurses, a white-haired, maiden lady with a wooden leg, who always wore her hairnet. I happened to be walking down the stairs one morning when I heard her call out from her room off the second floor landing. She needed help putting on her wooden leg, and of all people, she asked me!

CHAPTER THREE
ORANGE BASKETS AND SCRAMBLED EGGS

In our first year of training, we attended classes in Theory and Practice, taught by doctors, with the exception of Anatomy, taught by Nurse Davis. We also received instruction in hands-on patient care, taught by the nursing instructor. After our first year, we continued instruction under the supervision of the head nurse on our assigned units.

The physical therapist taught us how to administer a therapeutic back rub, and the dietician taught us how to prepare food for a patient's tray. I had never seen an "Orange Basket" and doubt if any of us had, until one day when we were in class, in her kitchen. A classmate, assigned with the task of making one for a breakfast tray, asked, in the most innocent tone, "But how do you do that? Put oranges in a basket?" Hearing that question, another classmate and I began to laugh! The dietician ordered us to stop, or leave the room, but the more we tried to stop, the more we laughed. Finally, I was able to control myself, but my friend had to walk out.

Class resumed, and we learned how to scoop out an orange to make it look like a fancy basket for fruit. I'm happy to report that the young woman who asked the question went on to attain a BS in Nursing and have a successful career.

Not long after the orange basket incident, my own lack of food-prep knowledge became the subject for laughter. Included in a head nurse's duties was the supervision of patients' meal service. The food was prepared in the main kitchen and transported to her unit on a steam cart for her to plate for serving on trays already set up by her unit's civilian kitchen maid, and delivered by nursing staff who returned them to the kitchen when meals were finished.

Occasionally, a head nurse assigned a trainee or staff member to prepare something special for a patient, in her unit's kitchen. One morning, I was assigned to make scrambled eggs. I had never made them before, but I had seen an RN prepare them and remembered how it was done. Or so I thought. The head nurse stood next to me at the stove and watched me break an egg into a small pan of water and begin to beat the mixture. I'll never forget the look on her face, as she attempted to contain her amusement. She asked what I was doing. I explained that I was making scrambled eggs. First she laughed, and then she taught me the right way. Her laughter was so genuine, and her manner so kindly, I didn't feel embarrassed for not knowing. I learned how to make scrambled eggs that day, but more importantly, I learned that I could laugh at myself.

I wasn't laughing, however, when I reported for duty in the dietician's kitchen one day, ready to prepare formula for newborns. After mixing the powdered formula with liquid, we poured it into sterilized, glass bottles and put the sterilized, rubber nipples on top. This assignment included leaving a supply of sterilized bottles and nipples for the next person. On this day, however, the nurse before me had ended her shift without doing so. I could not begin my work, until I finished hers.

The fact that someone would leave work undone was unthinkable. It made me mad, mad enough to report it to the dietician. After all, this was her department. She didn't say anything when I told her what had happened, but when I received my next performance evaluation, I discovered that she had labeled me, "Too Critical," because I had "complained" about the incident. That evaluation made me even madder; however, it never prevented me from continuing to notice what needed correcting, and alerting my supervisors. Sometimes I attended to it myself.

As our training progressed, and we mastered the art of making an Orange Basket, we moved on to the art of administering a bed bath, made all the more challenging, since there were no bathrooms or standing sinks with running water in patients' rooms. Before we could begin to bathe our patients, we had to go the utility room to get the water. Once more, my upbringing on Craney Hill came in handy. I was accustomed to carting water from the well and heating it on the woodstove, so the walk from a patient's room to the utility room was nothing. And the water was hot, right out of the faucet!

Learning to give a proper bed bath took practice, and like my fellow students, until I had the procedure down pat, I didn't always remember every step involved: First, remove the patient's gown and drape him or her by placing a folded, cotton flannel blanket over the bed sheet and bedspread, with its ends open at the top. Next, grasp the top of the blanket with one hand, holding it in place. With the other hand, take hold of the bottom of the blanket, along with the bed spread and sheet, and pulling them all down with one swoop, simultaneously remove the sheet and bedspread, and unfold the flannel blanket, which becomes a cover for the patient during the bath. When the bath is completed, remove the blanket.

While still a proby, I was assigned one morning to bathe a patient in the women's ward, and was surprised when a senior nurse, assigned to the same patient that evening, came up to me and asked, "Miss Morse, do you remember taking so-and-so's bath blanket off her during a.m. care?" In all seriousness, I answered, "Yes." "That's funny; it was still there when I gave p.m. care." We both laughed at my mistake. I never left a bath blanket on a patient again!

After we administered the bath and a back rub, we helped the patient into a fresh hospital gown, and then we made the bed. Proper bed making was another nursing art we learned to master. Until we did, the head nurse or our nursing instructor would rip out a saggy corner during inspections rounds, and make us start all over again. To conserve linens and cut down on laundering cost, we folded the top sheet and used it to cover the red, heavy rubber sheet protecting the middle section of the mattress. We never put soiled bed linen on the floor! Patients' pillows were feather-filled, covered with plain cotton ticking. We were instructed to place them on the beds with the open end of the pillowcase facing *away* from the door. Beds made and patients in fresh bed clothes, we cleaned the bedside table, placed a fresh glass of water or juice on it, and emptied and cleaned the urinal or bedpan.

In the wards, beds were separated from one another by a curtain hung from a ceiling track, which did little to provide patients with privacy. The legs of the beds had caster wheels, each caster with a metal lever that when stepped on, locked the wheel to keep the bed from moving. Aside from the general rules for maintaining patients' beds, we followed the rules of the head nurse whose unit we'd been assigned to.

It was common knowledge that during nap time in the men's ward on a certain head nurse's floor, the caster wheels on all of the beds had to be positioned *horizontally*. When it was time for her patients to take their naps, she ordered staff to lower the window shades, making certain they were level with the window sill. After naps, we raised the shades to the same level. Her rules seemed so trivial to us at the time, but we made sure we followed them. In the beginning, we thought she acted like an army colonel, but we came to realize that she had a heart of gold.

In addition to working on the wards, we assisted doctors and surgical staff in the operating room (OR) during surgery, cleaning up afterwards, then took the rubber, surgical gloves down to a room in the basement to prepare them for sterilization and re-use. After washing and rinsing them in the double, soap-stone sink, we hung them on a wooden rack to dry, first right-side out, then inside-out. Since it would take at least twenty-four hours for them to dry on both sides, the next shift continued the preparation. Prior to turning the gloves right-side out again, staff put them on a cloth towel to powder them, front and back, and then paired them. Finally, they placed them in a double-wrapped cloth package and delivered them to the OR, where they were sterilized in the auto-clave, with high pressure steam.

Before the existence of the recovery room, our post-op patients were kept in the OR, until the anesthesiologist determined they were free enough of the effects of the anesthetic to cough, swallow, and take care of their own vomitus. At that point, they were returned by stretcher to their own beds on the medical/surgical unit, where they were monitored by a nurse, most often, a student nurse. She had the added responsibility of caring for three or four medical or surgical patients in various stages of illness or recovery, located in different rooms on the floor.

Anti-emetics did not come into use until much later, so it was not uncommon for patients to vomit after surgery. Taking that into account, we added a flannel covered, rubber sheet at the head of the bed when making it. It was also not uncommon for a patient to return with a Foley Catheter, a soft, rubber tube, inserted into the bladder through the urethra, to drain the urine, which was collected in an empty, glass, intravenous (IV) bottle that sat under the patient's bed. Staff emptied the bottle every eight hours, careful not to kick it over during routine patient care, or when making beds.

Without the life-saving measures that have since become available, medical/surgical patients either recovered, and they were discharged, or they died. In either case, nurses were required to strip the beds, clean the bed springs and bed frame, wipe down the mattress and mattress covers and pillow, the bedside table and over-bed table, and make the beds, before returning to hands-on care of other patients. If we had any free time after that, we folded linen in the linen closet.

My perception of this period in nursing history is that doctors were doers. Nurses were helpers, handing the doctor the equipment he needed in the OR, while he performed surgery, or in a patient's room, as he changed a surgical dressing, or took out stitches. After he finished the procedure, he walked out the door and went on to the next patient. We were left to clean up the mess.

CHAPTER FOUR
RE-USE, MONITOR, AND REGULATE

The further along we progressed in our training, the more proficient we became at connecting what we were learning in our studies with the hands-on care we were administering to the patients on our assigned units, correlating prescribed treatment with a patient's diagnosis. The average census on a medical/surgical unit was twenty patients, and we had to be familiar with the diagnosis, treatment and status of each, if they called for assistance. We also needed the information, in case the nursing director phoned for an update on a particular patient. We dreaded having to answer her phone call, because we knew that her interest went beyond the patient's condition. She was testing us to make sure we had been listening with our brains during the change of shift report.

Without question, students were the main work force in the hospital. Assigned to the less desirable evening and late shifts, we mostly worked alone. With no one to share duties, little experience, and no RN to consult, it was sink or swim. I remember the first time I was left alone on an evening shift to administer p.m. care to all of my twenty patients. I took their temps, gave them their meds, and got water from the utility room to fill their basins, so they could wash their faces and hands, and brush their teeth. After returning the basins to the utility room to empty them, I went back to the unit, emptied and cleaned bedpans and urinals, and gave each patient a five minute back rub, before I finished hands-on patient care. But my responsibilities weren't over until I completed documentation on all of the patients I had cared for, and then relayed their status and individual needs to the on-coming night nurse.

Accomplishing everything that was required in the time allotted seemed like an impossible task, made even more so, because I felt I had to do everything perfectly. I was scheduled to go off-duty at 11:30 p.m., but I never finished until 1:30 the next morning. I hadn't yet learned how to see what I could do to make myself more efficient, and I certainly did not feel right about cutting corners. It would have been helpful if I had been able to talk about my dilemma with someone who could guide me, but it was not the norm for our nursing instructor to check and see if we were correctly practicing what we were learning, or if we were having difficulties managing our duties and responsibilities.

No matter what shift we worked, we routinely took patients' temperatures at scheduled times. Both oral and rectal thermometers were made of glass, with a small, mercury-filled bulb at one end. As the temperature rose, the mercury expanded, causing it to rise up the glass; marked gradations indicated the degrees. Each patient's thermometer rested on a cotton ball and was partially covered in alcohol, inside its own glass, tube-like container, labeled with the patient's name, room and bed numbers.

The tubes were kept in individual compartments, in a hand-held, stainless steel, carry rack. When it was time to check temps, we lifted the rack by the finger hole, at the top of center post, and carried it to the patients' rooms. After taking the temp, we wiped off the thermometer and returned it to its holder, then recorded the reading in a Temp Book, a small composition notebook with the patients' identifying information, for later entry in their charts.

It wasn't until after the patient had been discharged that we washed the thermometer with soap and water. But not hot water! The mercury would become destabilized, causing it to register at the highest temperature on the thermometer, and stay there. In that case, we would not be able to use it again. What we didn't know at the time was that mercury is toxic. If we dropped a thermometer and it broke, we just swept up the pieces of glass, along with the beads of mercury, and threw them in the trash!

Another of our hands-on duties was to administer an enema to pre-op patients. In these early days, it was a soap suds enema, or SSE, as we called it, made from left-over slivers of soap we collected from the rooms of discharged patients, and dissolved in a gallon of water. The solution was kept in the utility room, with the enema procedure tray that held a two-quart, metal enema can. Protruding from the bottom of the can was a turned-down, metal spout. Attached to the spout was a three-foot length of half-inch rubber tubing, with a metal clamp to regulate the enema's flow, and a two-inch, glass connecting tube, about a half-inch around.

Since both tubes were already in place, all that was left to assemble the equipment was to get a clean, rectal tube from its stainless steel container—we called it a boat—and attach it to the glass tube. To prepare the SSE, we poured a half-cup of the soapy mixture into the enema can and diluted it with two quarts of warm water, but not before we checked to make sure that the metal clamp on the rubber tube was closed.

The enema can had a hole in the top, through which we threaded a strip of gauze, so that we could hang it from a pole we wheeled into the patient's room, and set up at bedside. After we administered the enema, we returned the pole and enema procedure tray to the utility room, disconnected the rectal tube from the glass tube, washed it with soap and water, and put it aside. The enema can and its attached tubes remained on the tray as they were.

When we had accumulated enough rectal tubes to sterilize at one time, we boiled them on a two-burner, counter-top, gas stove. I can't count how many times they got over-cooked, and the putrid smell of burning rubber infiltrated the unit. No, that smell was not from our rubber-soled shoes, as we ran up and down the hospital corridors! And it is not the only unpleasant smell from my student days that still lingers.

When a surgical patient undergoes a colostomy, the end of the colon leading to the patient's rectum is closed off, and a piece of healthy colon is diverted to an artificial opening created in the abdominal wall. That opening, known as a stoma, becomes the exit point for the patient's feces. Today, colostomy bags collect the fecal matter, but the only recourse available in these early days of my career was to cover the stoma with a gauze dressing, changing it frequently. Since it wasn't a surgical dressing, which could only be removed by a doctor, I was allowed to replace it. We didn't have disposable, plastic gloves at the time, so I used my bare hands.

The first time I was assigned to a patient recovering from a colostomy, I was immediately reminded of how Mary and I would go down to our dark, damp cellar, with its dirt floor, climb into the bin, where our home-grown potatoes were stored, and pick out the rotten ones. The memory of their foul smell helped me, as I lifted the soiled gauze from my patient's stoma. Just like on the farm, I knew I had a job to do, and I did it. But this time, I didn't have Mary with me.

For some students, working alone at night, or working without supervision may not have been problematic. For many of us, however, the thought of facing a difficult or unfamiliar situation, alone, was cause for anxiety, if not downright fear. I can speak to that fact, from my own experience

Memorial's nursery, labor, delivery, and post-partum rooms were all on the hospital's second floor, but the only phone was in the chart room. I was working in the nursery one evening when a senior student, attending a patient in the labor room, rushed in to tell me that the woman was about to give birth, the doctor was waiting in the doctor's room, in the basement, and she had to go to the chart room to call him! I would have to stay in the labor room until the doctor arrived.

Left alone with the patient, I lifted her sheet to see the progress of the labor. To my horror, the baby was exiting the birth canal, with the umbilical cord wrapped tightly around his neck. He was blue! What to do? In seconds I thought of the scissors in my pocket: Could I? Should I cut the cord? Simultaneously, without thought, I untangled the tight cord and lifted the infant up by the ankles. The doctor and student nurse came into the room, as the baby cried. In that moment, I realized I was trembling.

The subject of fear has come up in many of the conversations I've had with my retired colleagues, and the one most commonly shared was of making a mistake, especially when we'd been assigned to dispense meds. One friend spoke of her near error when giving a vitamin to the wrong patient. Fortunately, her quick thinking saved her. Before the man could swallow, she retrieved it with her finger.

She remembers telling him, "Open your mouth!" as clearly as if it were today. And she remembers the fear she felt when she said it.

In our student days, in an effort to prevent mistakes, the hospital had a policy prohibiting the meds nurse from talking to anyone while she worked in the meds room, filling the glass medicine cups with prescribed pills and capsules.

After she dispensed the meds, she delivered them to her patients on a small enamel tray, used solely for that purpose. The tray also held a small enamel pitcher of water, which she poured into the empty cups for easy swallowing. When she'd completed her rounds, she took the glass cups back to the utility room and washed them with soap and water, the only preparation for their re-use.

Narcotics were among the meds we might have dispensed, and in the early 1940's, they only came in pill form. To liquefy the pill for injection, we put it in a tablespoon of water, placed the spoon on the pedestal of an alcohol lamp, about the size of a tea cup, and heated it over the flame. Eventually, liquid narcotics came packaged in little glass ampoules. All we did was break off the top of the ampoule, where indicated, and draw the liquid into a syringe. It helped to grasp the ampoule's top with a two-inch gauze pad, to prevent getting cut on its sharp edge.

If we were assigned to administer an injection of regular insulin, we first had to check the patient's urine for sugar levels to determine the amount of insulin required. Four times a day, once before each meal and at bedtime, we collected a specimen and took it to the utility room for testing. Using a medicine dropper, we removed eight drops of the urine, deposited them into an empty, glass test tube, and added five cubic centimeters (cc) of Benedict's Solution, a reagent used to determine the presence of sugar. Heating the mixture over a Bunsen Burner for one minute was enough time for the heat to change the color of the liquid. We were able to determine the sugar level by comparing the color in the tube with the corresponding color on a chart: Clear blue or green indicated an absence of sugar; light, greenish yellow, a faint trace; yellow to orange, a moderate amount; chocolate brown or brick-red, more than two per cent.

Orders for the corresponding amount of regular insulin would have been prescribed and recorded by the patient's physician, so once we had the level, we drew up the correct amount of insulin into the syringe. Long after my student days, glucose strips simplified testing for sugar levels. We simply immersed a strip into a urine specimen, observed as it changed color, and compared that color with the chart to determine the amount of insulin needed.

The syringes were comprised of glass barrels and plungers, with detachable, stainless steel needles. When it was time to sterilize them, we boiled them together, on the same two-burner, counter top stove we used to cook the enema tubes. Friction from frequent boiling caused burrs to develop on the needles. Another of our tasks was to sharpen them, periodically, on a whetstone. Burrs hurt!

In this same time period, only a doctor was allowed to start an IV. The attending nurse was responsible for monitoring the IV, but since there were no established guidelines for regulating flow, 1000 cc, the equivalent of a quart of fluid, might run into the patient's vein, over a three hour period. It wasn't until the early 1950's, when set rates were finally established, that the rapid administration of fluid, or blousing, was no longer a common occurrence. There were set rates in the 1940's, however, for oxygen flow when patients received oxygen therapy, and nurses not only monitored it; we administered it.

In our hospital, until the introduction of Penicillin in the early 1940's, the two mainstays for treating Pneumonia were oxygen therapy and quality nursing. Assigned to a Pneumonia patient requiring oxygen, I first raised the bed to a comfortable, upright position, and then I set up the isinglass and canvas oxygen tent, which would enclose the patient's head and torso. I checked it for rips, mending any with tape. If the tent was equipped with a separate ice chamber, oxygen passing over the ice provided moisture, like a humidifier. I was also responsible for monitoring the melted ice that

26

accumulated in the collection pan. We didn't have a housekeeping department, so I mopped up any spills.

When I completed my preparations, I went out into the hall to get the 148 lb oxygen tank the boiler man would have brought up from the basement, on a carrier. After I pushed it next to the patient's bedside, I set up the connecting hose that would deliver the prescribed liters of oxygen per minute, from the tank to the tent, and with a wrench, fastened the gauge for monitoring flow. Finally, I secured the tent and opened the valve on the tank to begin therapy. If the patient required additional oxygen, the boiler man would leave another full tank in the hall, ready for me to push next to the almost empty one. I'd remove the gauge from the first tank, and install it on the new one.

My first Pneumonia patient was a woman with beautiful, black hair she wore in two long braids. In addition to administering and monitoring her oxygen therapy, I fed her and bathed her, helped her on and off the bedpan, and brushed and re-braided her hair. Following the dictates of good medical judgment for the time, it was my duty to conserve her strength, as well as alleviate her symptoms. If she was sleeping, I did not wake her to take her temp. When she was allowed visitors, I instructed them to refrain from making it necessary for her to talk. With treatment, rest, and care, she was able to recover.

One Pneumonia patient on my assigned unit, however, remained gravely ill, in spite of all the measures available, including Penicillin. The year was 1946. I was working in the unit's meds room one day, when her physician, Dr. Barton, arrived, carrying his medical bag. I can still see him, a jovial man with a spry step, as he walked in, opened the bag, and handed me a vial, explaining that it was Streptomycin, a new drug he hoped would cure his patient. He gave me instructions for mixing a multi-dose vial, and then gave the dosage I was to draw up into a syringe for an immediate injection. Dr. Barton also wrote out orders for continued dosages and times.

I filled the syringe and went along on my own to inject the patient with her first dose of this newest wonder drug. I remember feeling that something important was happening when I walked into her room to administer the first injection of Streptomycin in our hospital. It was an honor for me, as a student, to have a part in it. By the next afternoon, the young woman was on her way to recovery. I'll never forget her smile when she realized she'd be going home soon.

CHAPTER FIVE
LET THE REBELLIONS BEGIN!

Authoritative is the best description for the style of nursing management we were accustomed to during training, and beyond. The head nurse was the boss. Whether as students or staff assigned to her unit, we asked her permission before acting on anything besides the most basic, hands-on care. We didn't even go off-duty at our scheduled time, until we received it

Students never questioned assignments, and we certainly did not feel free to request being assigned to a patient whose disease and treatment we wanted to learn more about. Personal confrontation with staff was not encouraged. With superiors, it was unthinkable.

We had rules to live and work by, but that doesn't mean I always followed them, exactly. One of my earliest rebellions was of little consequence and didn't last long. When I worked the night shift, after eight hours with no time to eat or drink, my mouth tasted like the bottom of a canary cage. Occasionally, I chewed gum to freshen my breath, well aware that I was breaking a hospital rule. I was giving my change of shift report to the day head nurse one morning, when she stopped me. "Miss Morse, are you chewing gum?" Swallowing hard, I replied, "No," and continued with my report.

Another student rebellion took place on the Pediatric Unit. Hospital rules required us to put on a gown and wear a mask, while administering care to patients who had contagious diseases, and were placed on precaution. I was on the night shift, working alone, and about to take the rectal temperature of a child placed on precaution when I decided that I wouldn't gown up. *I'm not picking the child up and holding him. I'm just going to take his temperature and wash my hands when I'm done. I'm not going to touch anything else. Why do I need to gown up?* Gownless, I proceeded to insert the thermometer at the very moment the night supervisor was making her rounds. I was caught! From then on, I put on my mask and gown.

Two of my more dramatic rebellions did not take place in my home hospital. In 1946, Memorial Hospital corporately merged with Margaret Pillsbury Hospital. Each would remain a separate entity, with its own nursing school and residence, but their affairs would be conducted by a single administrator. Until they physically merged in one location, establishing the new Concord Hospital, they would be known as the Memorial Unit and the Margaret Pillsbury Unit of Concord Hospital, and staff and students from each would float between the two.

Before this arrangement, there had been little contact between Memorial and Pillsbury students and staff, a factor that contributed to our displeasure with the new policy. We didn't appreciate having to walk several blocks, in all kinds of weather, to get from one place to another, but our biggest upset was the fact that we would not know which of the hospitals we'd been assigned to, until we reported for our shift. As time went on and more people expressed their dissatisfaction with floating, I realized that I was not the only one who did not want to leave the familiarity of *my hospital.*

My first rebellion at Margaret Pillsbury took place on its Annex I, with private rooms for elite patients, and a head nurse who treated them as if they were guests in a fancy hotel. She expected the staff and students she supervised to do the same. If one of her patients

29

wanted a cup of tea, it was our duty to go to the unit's kitchen and make it. We did not make tea for any of our other patients!

Given the assignment one day, I stood in the unit's kitchen, about to pour water into a patient's tea cup, when the assistant head nurse walked in. Without a word, she took the kettle out of my hand. Dumbfounded, I stepped aside. "Well, if you think I can't make a cup of tea, you do it! I'm going home!"

I have no idea what might have motivated my superior to take the kettle from me in the first place, but I do know her action made me feel incapable, a feeling I was not accustomed to. And it made me angry. I can still see the shocked look on her face, as she handed the kettle back. I made the tea. Nothing was ever said about the encounter. I was probably the first student who had ever stood up to her, and she never did anything like that to me again.

Hospital stays could last for weeks, even months, so many of the female patients arrived on this unit with suitcases full of dainty lingerie, bed jackets and robes, the likes of which I had never seen or felt in my life. It wasn't unusual for them to bring their jewelry, too. When we admitted them, we were required to make a list of all their possessions, before carefully placing them in closets and drawers. In my mind, it was an awful duty—not what I went into nursing for. Wasted time!

Another time-wasting duty, not limited to this unit, resulted from the commonly held belief that flowers took up too much oxygen when left at a bedside overnight. We stored them in the utility room, where the cooler temperature kept them fresh, but before we returned them in the morning, we changed the water in the vase, removed any dead blooms, and rearranged the bouquet.

I felt that performing this duty for the elite patients on Annex I contributed to an expectation that everyone on staff was there to do nothing else but serve them, in any way their hearts desired. I had a hard time holding my tongue and acting properly, the manner expected of a nurse, especially a student nurse, when I was assigned there, and might have been kicked out of training, if I had been reported on the morning I finally reached my tolerance level.

The moment I entered a female patient's room, she greeted me with, "I'll have my flowers brought in now. Put this here and that there, and then I'd like my breakfast." I was bug-eyed to think someone was treating me like that! I responded in a nasty-sweet voice, "I am not wearing a black and white uniform. My uniform is blue and white." Then, I turned on my one-and-a-half inch heels and walked out of the room.

One of my most liberating student rebellions didn't take place in either of the hospitals. A few days before a scheduled, free weekend, my friend from Henniker and I were looking forward to going home, until someone in our residence disobeyed the house rule explicitly stating that sanitary napkins could not be discarded "in the hopper under any circumstances!" Everyone in the residence was campused, because the person responsible did not come forward.

I felt the punishment was unjust and said so to my friend. "I'm not staying here all weekend! Are you?" So we came up with a plan. When Friday morning arrived, we got hold of our boyfriends and told them to come pick us up that night. They were to park the car between the residence and the hospital at 10:00 p.m., and we would meet them, after lights-out.

The housemother flashed her light into our rooms during her bed check that night, unaware that my friend and I were lying, fully clothed, under the covers, ready to make our escape. Satisfied to find us where we belonged, she returned to the living room on the first floor, our signal that it was safe for us to stuff our beds with pillows to make it look like we were sleeping, and meet out in the hall. Like mice, we crept along to the back stairs, then down and out the side door, and into the waiting car. We didn't give much thought to the consequences of our actions, not even when we managed to sneak back on Sunday afternoon without being caught.

One of our upper-class residents, however, wasn't as lucky. All students were issued four late passes a month, which entitled us to stay out until 11:30 p.m., an hour-and-a half beyond curfew. This unfortunate student got caught trying to sneak back to her room after 10:00 p.m., without her late pass. Knowing she couldn't get back into the residence by going through the front door, she decided to sneak in by way of Memorial's pediatric unit, which was connected to our building by an enclosed, wooden walk-way.

Her plan was to climb the fire escape outside the unit's window, and when she got inside, go down the stairs that led to the wooden walkway, cross it into the nurses' residence, then walk up the stairs to her room. All of this without being seen. But the nursing supervisor who had caught me taking temps without my mask and gown was making her rounds on the pediatric unit, and just happened to be standing at the window, as the unlucky student climbed in from the fire escape. No more late passes for her that month.

Although there may have been times when I acted before I thought about the consequences of my actions, I can say that there was one time I did think first, and with good reason. Working the night shift in the women's ward, on Margaret Pillsbury's second floor, I passed the open door of that unit's kitchen, and saw Miss Fitzgerald, our night supervisor, sitting upright in the straight-back chair she had pulled up to the open, oven door of the gas stove. Her head tipped to one side, she had obviously fallen asleep in her attempt to warm up after walking the hospital's drafty, high-ceilinged corridors. It was comical to see the prim and proper Fitzie, as we called her behind her back, in that position. But I knew better than to laugh. I didn't want to be the one to wake her, so I walked away, chuckling to myself. Best to stay clear of Fitzie's wrath.

CHAPTER SIX
SURVIVAL IN THE PRESENCE OF SUFFERING

In 1947, half-way through my training, I seriously considered leaving. Nothing in our studies had prepared us for the three months we would spend as affiliate students in the New Hampshire State Hospital for the Mentally Ill (NHSH). The institution felt like a place where people were sent with no expectation that they would return to their lives. During my entire rotation, I never saw any of the patients I came in contact with get well, or go home. They just walked around, looking as if they were lost. Nothing to do. No place to go. No end in sight.

Before the use of medication, standard treatment for mental illness included Shock Therapy, which induced seizures, and Continuous Cold Tub Therapy, which caused a slow-down of blood-flow to the brain, resulting in decreased mental and physical activity.

During Electrical Shock Therapy, the seizures were induced by placing several electrodes on the patient's scalp and applying an electrical current. With Insulin Shock Therapy, they were created by administering large doses of insulin to lower the patient's blood glucose level. For chemically induced Shock Therapy, the patient was injected with Metrazol, a circulatory and respiratory stimulant that causes convulsions when administered in large doses. Sometimes all three forms of Shock Therapy were combined.

Patients receiving Continuous Cold Tub Therapy were immersed in a tub of cold water. Placed over the tub, and secured, was a heavy canvas sheet, with a hole for the patient's head. The treatment could last for several hours, and although I never encountered it on my shifts, I was told that it might be extended for several days.

Few of us had ever been able to talk about our rotation at NHSH. Left alone on its wards to fend for ourselves, we had no one to help us with what we might be feeling. However, a few years ago, a friend and former colleague, the late Georgina Green Hurd, had invited a group of nurses, some still working at Concord Hospital, to get together and share our stories about nursing. At the time, Georgina was writing a book, *Lantern on the Stern,* about her career, and had devoted a chapter to NHSH. Hearing her share the account of her own experience allowed us to break the silence about our own.

I regret to say that Georgina died before her book was published. I was saddened by her death. I was also saddened and disappointed to learn that her sister could find no trace of the manuscript, after the death of Georgina's husband. Fortunately, Georgina had given me a copy of the chapter about NHSH, during our gathering. In honor of her years of service and her efforts to help other nurses remember and tell their stories, perhaps for the first time, I am including excerpts from it:

***

With the Advantage of Hindsight: A Long Look Back at the Psychiatric Affiliation at the State Hospital in 1947.

> *There was not a graduate or Registered Nurse on any of the floors to which we were assigned, except the Head Nurse [...] Thus we were given assignments and set adrift each day to do with them whatever was our best effort, with little supervision or mentoring attention. [...] we had not been learning 'psychiatric nursing,' we had been learning 'warehousing.' We had been losing out on the benefits of 'continuity of care,' on help learning how to talk beneficially with disturbed or at-risk patients, but we instead responded to unspoken 'rules' not to talk with patients. [...] We were fortunate on the day of our meeting that some few of us had been in the State Hospital training later than the rest of us, and they had seen the beginning of medication with anti-psychotics so that we could change our opinions of the hopelessness [....]*

I believe without exception we all remembered fear with which we suffered when assigned to certain areas, certain floors, certain therapies, the fear at passing the 'Isolation Rooms' and the instruction about not ever letting a patient be behind us. The therapy areas, such as 'ECT,' (electroshock therapy), 'Tub (Continuous Bath ('CB's'), Insulin Shock Therapy, and Metrozal [sic] Therapy. [...] Fear of the responsibility of of various kinds of damage to the patient, due to the administration of the therapy, or assistance with it. We also remembered the frustration of having to do these treatments, with no understanding of their purpose nor the outcomes, which we had never seen as beneficial, in part because of the lack of continuity of contact with the patient...we suffered also from the lack of positive reinforcement....'

***

It wasn't until I had gone back to Georgina's writing, before beginning my own, that I realized how much I had not allowed myself to remember about my affiliation at NHSH. The more I wrote, the more clearly I recalled watching the terrible shaking patients experienced, while undergoing Shock Therapy. But I still could not picture what I did to assist the doctors. Recently, during a conversation with another retired, fellow affiliate, the subject of our duties came up, and she reminded me that one of them was to place a padded throat stick into patients' mouths to prevent them from biting off their tongues, during the seizures.

For all that I could not remember about NHSH, an incident on an open ward for female psychiatric patients remains as vivid in my memory as the day it happened. I was working alone when suddenly, one of the ambulatory patients came after me with a heavy, oak rocking chair. She was very tall, so the chair was about to come down on me with great force. To defend myself, I did the only thing I could think of. I grabbed the chair in mid-air and turned its direction, causing the patient to spin away from me. Not only had there been no staff present to help me, I don't remember seeing someone in authority I could report the incident to.

The most surprising memory to surface from this affiliation is of me voicing my frustration and anger, during a conversation in the small living room of our affiliates' residence. At the end of a shift one evening, a few of us had gotten together to relax and talk about how our day had gone. At some point in the conversation, I turned to our house mother, seated at her desk, and began telling her how I hated working on the Psychiatric Wards, because I couldn't stand to see how the patients were treated. I felt it was inhumane. They were fed like animals. And the way they drank out of cups that looked like children's teapots, holding the spouts to their mouths. All I could feel was disgust.

The house mother tried to calm me down by telling me the conditions weren't as bad as I was making them out to be. That made me furious. I got up from my chair and stood, facing her across her desk. "Have you ever worked over there to see what I am talking about?" None of the other students disagreed with me. The housemother said no more.

I had gotten it off my chest. It didn't help. And it didn't change anything. Improvements in psychiatric care at New Hampshire State Hospital would not be made until well after we had graduated and were working as career nurses.

Following my three month rotation at NHSH, I was assigned to a second affiliation in the Department of Pediatrics at Bellevue Hospital in New York City. Memorial Hospital did not have enough pediatric patients to provide its trainees with experience in Pediatric Theory and Practice, so it sent us there, in groups of three and four, until our entire class completed the requirements.

Before our arrival, Bellevue had sent out letters informing prospective affiliates and their parents of the hospital's rules and regulations. I was not surprised that we were required to attend classes and work on the wards, as we had at Memorial, but it was surprising to learn that we would be assigned late passes more frequently, and with them, we could stay out until midnight.

In early fall of 1947, I left Concord, New Hampshire with three of my classmates and set out for New York, New York. Everything about the trip is a blur. I vaguely remember a huge train station and a great deal of activity. All those people moving around in groups reminded me of a flock of sheep.

We were assigned rooms in our residence, across the street from the hospital, a big, tall building with so many corridors, so many directions to take. Getting to the classrooms on the eighth floor was a scary experience for me. I had been on elevators before, but I'd never gone up as high as that. On our first day of classes, I was so afraid the elevator might break down, I walked up the eight flights. After that I decided, *It's not worth the effort, so I'll ride from here on.*

My first work assignment was on the pediatric tuberculosis (TB) unit, caring for children ranging in age from nine months to four years. The large, open ward was filled with rows of cribs lined up against the walls, as well as in the center of the space, and all of them were occupied. The cribs had handrails on the sides, but no nets on top, and I was surprised to see that many of the mattresses were without sheets; most likely they were in short supply. I wasn't accustomed to seeing bare mattresses at Memorial. It didn't take long before it became apparent that I would see and experience many things at Bellevue that I was not accustomed to.

I had gotten over my resistance to gowning up and wearing a mask to take care of patients on precaution at Memorial, and as a result, I wasn't afraid that I would catch any of the infectious diseases I had been exposed to, like Polio. I soon found out, however, that Bellevue did not provide us with gowns and masks. Realizing that I would be working without the protection I had become accustomed to, I became afraid of catching TB when taking the children's temps.

During the course of a shift, we took rectal temps every three or four hours and were required to hold the mercury-filled, glass thermometer in place for three minutes to allow the mercury time to register an accurate reading. Three minutes is a long time; and these kids were coughing.

Exposure to disease wasn't my only concern. How could I get all of my duties completed by the end of my shift, if I had to hold the thermometer for three minutes, for every child with a previously recorded, elevated temp? I remember thinking how impossible it was, and that I wanted to go back home. But I didn't know the way, so I had to stick it out.

After about a month on this ward, I was on night duty with an affiliate student from another hospital, and even though we shared the work load, we both knew we couldn't take rectal temps the required way and finish our work on time. That's when my co-worker came up with a short cut. I watched as she placed her hand on the children's foreheads, guessed what degree their temperatures might be, and recorded that number. At first, I thought, *I don't like to do this,* but I let go of my objection when I realized that she was going to get her share of the work done, long before I did. So, I followed her example. However, if we found a child we suspected had a fever, or if we had a question after checking an earlier reading, we took the temp.

The wide open space of the pediatric tuberculosis unit allowed us to see the children in their cribs from any vantage point, but because the area was so large, it took time to get from one point to another. My most vivid memory of my work there is watching as a little boy, perhaps four years old, climbed to the top of the rail on his crib and stood up. I couldn't believe my eyes. I heard the child's skull crack as he hit the floor. Like a pumpkin. I was too far away to prevent the fall. My co-worker wasn't near enough, either. She and I both ran, but by the time we reached him, he was already unconscious. I stayed with him while she went for help.

After we watched the child being taken away, we went back to our duties, as if nothing had happened. I don't remember either of us

38

saying a word. There was no opportunity to talk to a counselor about what we might be feeling, and it never occurred to me to approach our supervisor. No one in authority approached me. People didn't talk in those days. Families didn't talk, especially in front of the children. It was what we were accustomed to.

All I know is that child was somebody's little boy, and I couldn't save him. I still wonder what might have happened if he had fallen during the day shift. With more staff on duty, would someone have been close enough to catch him? Or grab hold of him, before he fell?

The Bellevue rotation also included the opportunity to work on a medical unit, caring for children who suffered from Spina Bifida, Cleft Palate, and other physical abnormalities and diseases I had not encountered at Memorial. On this unit, I took care of a young girl named Star, whose congenital abnormality interfered with her ability to swallow. Feeding tubes were not in use at the time, so we attempted to feed her by mouth.

I felt helpless when I tried to feed Star, a different kind of helplessness from what I had felt with that little boy. I had been unable to save him, but if he had died, as I suspected he had, then he no longer had to suffer. Star was still alive, and I wanted to fix her. But nothing I did could change her fate. That little girl's suffering would continue for as long as she lived.

We were taught to be helpers. "Give, Give, Give!" But we were kids ourselves, for heavens' sake, going about our days with little, if any, support. We learned to mask our feelings and live by the unspoken rule, "Just put up with, and do the best you can."

CHAPTER SEVEN
BELLEVUE WASN'T ALL WORK

I no longer remember a doctor or nurse at Bellevue, by name, or who taught our classes, but I clearly remember the little kitchen adjoining the pediatric tuberculosis unit. One of my more pleasant memories of the hospital is standing in that kitchen and eating thin, raisin cookies; they called them biscuits. I'd never had them before. Oh My Goodness! The raisins were all ground up so you wouldn't know you were eating raisins. This farm girl had grown up on home-made stuff, but those biscuits were delicious. I still see them and can almost taste them, after all this time.

Tucked in next to the kitchen, was the meds closet, an even smaller area. Among the meds stored and prepared for dispensing were glass vials of Penicillin, in powder form. Before the antibiotic could be injected, it had to be reconstituted by mixing it with saline. A posted sign stated, "When you need the Penicillin mixed, call a resident." The first time I was assigned to meds duty and read it, I thought to myself, *Why call a resident when I can mix it myself?*

I had mixed Penicillin enough times at Memorial to know that after I lifted off the metal cover on the multi-dose, glass vial of the powder, I would have to inject the saline into its metal rimmed, rubber top, making certain that I had the correct number of cc, in proportion to the number of units of powder. But it wasn't until I went on duty one night and discovered I needed Penicillin, that I had my chance. Rather than call for help, I mixed the drug and got away with it.

Differences in the way things were done at Bellevue weren't limited to how and when we worked and studied; they included the frequency of our days off, and how we spent them. At Memorial, we were accustomed to a work/class schedule that added up to a forty-eight hour week, but at Bellevue, it was only forty hours. As for how we spent our weekends off, we were too far away to go home, but we had plenty of activities to occupy our free time. The hospital not only organized extra-curricular programs for our benefit, it also provided recreational facilities, including tennis courts. We were even permitted to use the roof of our residence for sunbathing, but because of the proximity to the hospital and other public buildings, we were encouraged to be "selective" about where we chose to locate our blankets and towels.

According to the Bellevue's handbook for affiliate students, we were expected to be "governed by the dictates of good taste in the matter of neatness and suitability of dress." If we weren't certain what that meant, we were invited to discuss the matter with the director of student personnel. The hospital's policy of no slacks or shorts in the dining room was the same as Memorial's, but we weren't required to have "presentable hair" in our residence, as we had been back home. We were required, however, to be "fully clothed" when passing through, or answering the phone in the corridor on our floor.

Television sets were not available yet, but we were allowed radios, only after we registered them; among the reasons listed for that requirement was so that we could receive our radio regulations. I spent most of my off-duty hours in my room, embroidering or writing letters to people back home, until lights-out. Embroidery helped take my mind off what I saw every day, working on the wards; the pretty colors of the threads made me feel good. Knowing that I could create something beautiful and useful, and do it well, gave me a sense of accomplishment.

By the time I had left for my rotation at Bellevue, I had become engaged to Malcolm McComish, the boyfriend who had waited outside the residence at Memorial, the night my roommate and I escaped. During our courtship, I had become acquainted with his sister, Gretchen, about three or four years older than me, and wrote to her while I was at Bellevue. I had forgotten about our correspondence, until I was cleaning out her desk, after her death a few years ago, and found two of my letters. I had come to know that my sister-in-law never threw anything away, but that didn't lessen my surprise when I found the letters, still in their original envelopes. Reading them after all that time, I was even more surprised to be reminded that I had done more than embroider and write home when I was off-duty at Bellevue.

In my letter dated, Sunday, October 5, 1947, I wrote that my classmates and I had finished half of the course and had our final test, a stiff exam we had to study hard for. I mentioned one of the girls in our group who really got to me. She thought she was the only one who knew everything, and I wanted to get a higher mark than she got. I did.

I also told Gretchen that it was a good thing my fellow affiliates and I didn't stay longer than three months in New York, or we'd all probably be penniless. Still, we might as well enjoy ourselves while we could. For the remainder of the letter, I painted quite a picture of how I'd spent some of my off-duty time.

***

[…] Today was one of my two days off-- went up to Fifth Avenue this afternoon and watched a Polish parade. They were dressed in the Polish costume- and there were bands, etc. Something like our Memorial Day program- Tonight we heard about it on the news over the radio.

Last night another girl and I went to a Polish Community dance and had a wonderful time-I danced Polish polkas and they aren't anything like ours. I love to dance anyway. Concord and Henniker are going to seem a little dark and quiet I imagine, but I'll be glad to get back to them… I'll try to write again- time for 'light's out.' Will I ever be glad when the day comes that I can turn them off-whenever I get ready to.

Love, Bertha

***

Standing at Gretchen's desk, reading words I had written over sixty years before, I began to recall details I hadn't included in the letter. I guess I had decided at the time that I wasn't going to tell her

42

everything that had happened. She was Malcolm's sister, after all. For obvious reasons, I had left out the part about the mature, short, stout, white haired man at the community dance. I remembered thinking, when he came over and asked me to dance the Polka, *Why not? He knows how, and I don't. I'll learn from him, and then I'll be all set for the young fellows!* He was a wonderful dancer and good leader, and I couldn't help but follow him.

Later that night I did get to dance with a young guy. Oh, yes! He was red headed and nice looking. He was a gentleman. When the dance was over and we were all ready to leave, he asked if he could take me home. I told him I couldn't do that. But I did go out with somebody else another time. We met at one of the dances. I hadn't seen him before and was surprised when he came over to ask me to dance. I jumped at the chance. He told me his name was Jack. I told him my name was Ruth.

Jack thought I was pretty cool. If I hadn't been engaged, I would have thought he was pretty cool, too. Jack asked if he could take me out sometime, and I said he could. He came to the nurses' residence to get me, and we walked to Central Park. I didn't know Central Park was so big! We just walked. I don't remember what we saw. As the evening went on, I looked at my watch and realized that I should be getting back. I started running. "I have to be home!" "I gotta go! We gotta go!" Jack called out, "That's the wrong way!" We got back in time, but I have no idea how we got there.

In the second letter to Gretchen, dated October 27, 1947-Monday Evening, I told her that I had worked the night before and that my friend and classmate from Henniker had awakened me to give me her letter, so I could read it before I went to class:

***

It was almost like having breakfast in bed-only I think I enjoyed your letter more than I would breakfast [...] Sounds as though everyone was

43

getting engaged or married at home. My sister really surprised me. I didn't expect it so soon.

I have taken quite a few pictures with my camera since we've been here, some of the building and the street near the nurses' home & the hospital. I'll have to show them to you when we get home-so you'll have some idea of the 'dump' we've been working & living in.

People live so differently out here-we think nothing of walking up dirty old streets lined with 'bums' either on the steps or just propped up against a building. The other night we saw a man who had evidently been hit by a car, lying flat on his face-covered with blood. The things we see are almost unbelievable. It really is like looking at pictures in Life *magazine. The other night we saw a large mob of Communists-and the other day we saw a man walking up and down in front of a building-wearing a sign that said,* WORKERS ON STRIKE. *It seems strange to* see *things that we* read *about back home.*

My roommate and I went out to New Rochelle two weeks ago to visit a friend's parents. It seemed so good to get away from here & to see some grass and trees.

I guess I didn't tell you- someone sent us the new Concord Hospital 'dust caps.' I suppose they think we are wearing them here, but if they are, they're very wrong. I'd like to see the day when we do!

Last Friday, we had our hair fixed. I had mine cut, trimmed, thinned, shampooed & set for $1.50. It really looks a lot better and is a lot easier to take care of. Looks like I've come to the end of my Line- so until next time-Love, Bertha

***

Discovering my letters to Gretchen allowed me to relive a long-forgotten part of my life, the excitement of the dances, the unimaginable sights I witnessed on the streets of New York. I had never seen anyone back home whose skin color was different from mine. I had no idea that people gathered in mobs or walked in picket lines, carrying signs, no awareness this sort of thing was happening in our country. I doubt if anyone else from home knew, either.

Reading what I had written about those new, awful looking, "dust caps" that Memorial had sent, I felt upset all over again. My fellow affiliates and I got angry when we learned that we were expected to wear them, and not just while we were at Bellevue.

We had proudly worn our home hospital's stiff, white caps, with the two, black velvet, quarter-inch stripes we had earned. But these new, oval-shaped, un-starched caps, without stripes, looked like something you'd wear cleaning house. They had no meaning for us. It hurt to have the caps that had been a symbol of our achievement taken away from us. Well, we did not wear those dust caps during the remainder of our rotation in New York. No, no, we did not do that.

I had a good laugh, when I read what I had written to Gretchen about taking the train ride to New Rochelle, especially when I started recalling some of the details I had left out. It had been a beautiful autumn day, early in our rotation at Bellevue, and my roommate and I were on our way to visit a fellow student's family. We had never gone to New Rochelle and had no idea how long it would take to get there.

We'd been traveling for a while when the train stopped, and the doors on either side of the passenger car opened. Thinking we had arrived at our destination, we went out the door on the left side. The stop didn't last long, and when the train pulled away, we found ourselves on a platform in the middle of the tracks, with no place to go. Fortunately, another train came by within minutes. We boarded, and when it stopped at the New Rochelle station, we knew enough to step out through the door on the right side of the car, and onto the station's platform.

I can't recall how we got from the station to our friend's house, but I'll never forget the lunch her mother provided for us, the most delicious sandwiches with tomatoes from her garden. Every

September since, I think of that treat, two slices of store-bought bread with mayonnaise. Oh my, yes! We never had mayonnaise at home. We put sugar on tomatoes.

As for getting my hair fixed, I'm certain that when Gretchen read about my visit to the hair dresser, she would not have needed an explanation. Women didn't have their hair "done" in the 1940's; they had it "fixed." The place I went to in New York was ritzy, no little, cheap place. And a man cut my hair! I'd never had a man cut my hair before. It looked really nice, and made me feel special. It was not a feeling we had in our daily lives.

The affiliation at Bellevue ended in time for us to be home for Thanksgiving. I was glad to be done with it. Glad to be back. But now I had to remember that I wasn't Ruth anymore. I just had to be me.

CHAPTER EIGHT
WELCOME HOME?

One of the positive aspects of our rotation at Bellevue was that we worked for an extended period of time in the same location. Consistently knowing where to report for duty relieved some of the apprehension we felt about the challenges we might face during a shift. But returning to Concord meant going back and forth between the Memorial and Margaret Pillsbury Units, not knowing which of the two we would work in that day, until we reported for duty. And to make matters worse, we had to wear those new caps.

Resentment about the floating policy, which had been building before we went away, was even stronger now that we were back. In the end, we had to accept it. But we did raise a ruckus about the caps and eventually got them changed. Unfortunately, we could not prevent the hospital from putting a design of that ugly, dust cap on the commemorative pin we received at graduation. You know, I've since lost that pin, and I don't really care.

In the last six months of training, we were given the opportunity to choose our area of specialization; that choice determined whether we would be assigned to Memorial or Margaret Pillsbury. All during the time I was working on Memorial's medical/surgical unit, I had been observing how the head nurse ran her unit. She was the one responsible for making decisions. She was in charge. Realizing I wanted that for myself, I chose to specialize in Management. Happily, my choice meant I could remain at Memorial, *my* hospital.

In September of 1948, I joined all of the graduate nursing students in New Hampshire, as we assembled at the State House of Representatives in Concord to take the State Board Exams. After I'd finished answering all of the questions, I looked up to discover that I was the last person in the room. I didn't care. Several months later, I got the test results, and felt that the time I had taken to complete the test had been worth it.

Once I received the Certificate of Verification, stating that I had passed the State Boards, I could proudly write the letters, "RN" after my name. I had reached my goal. Oh, and by the way, those letters would also entitle me to receive a twenty dollar increase in my monthly salary.

Our graduating class received congratulatory letters and telegrams from our teachers, mentors, and hospital administrators, as well as from the superintendants of private and public schools in Concord, the editor of the city's two daily newspapers, the mayor, and the governor.

Mayor Charles McKee, speaking for the citizens of Concord, wrote to express appreciation of our choice of a career in nursing:

***

"[…] Your contribution to the health and welfare of this community, or such other in which you may elect to practice, is

47

of inestimable value in maintaining our American standards of life...."

***

Governor Charles M. Dale of New Hampshire wrote in his telegram:

"[...] NEW HAMPSHIRE NEVER HAD A GREATER NEED FOR WELL TRAINED NURSES. NOT ALONE FOR THEIR PROFESSIONAL SKILL [...] BUT BECAUSE OF THEIR ABILITY TO CONTRIBUTE TO GOOD CITIZENSHIP."

***

We felt proud to receive recognition for all our hard work, from people in high places, and we were pleased to accept it. But we were even more pleased with ourselves.

After graduation, I took a week off from my nursing duties, fully expecting to return in my new capacity as staff nurse on the medical/surgical unit of Memorial Hospital, where I had spent the six months of my specialization. On my first day back, I reported to work at Memorial, only to be told to report to the Margaret Pillsbury Unit! I was furious. I thought I was out from under the floating policy. As a student, I had no choice but to go along, but as a paid employee, I believed I had the right and responsibility to make my own decisions about where I worked.

I was boiling when I told my superior, "If I had known this would happen, I wouldn't have come back here." All tied up in my emotions, I didn't register her response. I did report to the Margaret Pillsbury Unit that day, as assigned, but the next day I returned to my unit at Memorial, and stayed.

My duties as a staff nurse were not all that different from those I had performed as a student, and neither was the way I performed them. I continued to make certain that patients received care that met with the highest standard, and it wasn't long before I came upon a clear example of what I believed did not meet that standard.

A young man, whose arms and hands were completely bandaged, was unable to wash his private parts, after his care-givers had administered a bed bath. He had gone for days in that circumstance, before I was assigned to him. When I realized what had been happening, I knew I could not let him continue like that. Covering him so he would not feel embarrassed, I washed him with great respect. Although we never spoke of what I had done, I knew he was grateful. I don't recall if I said something to the head nurse about how long he had gone without proper care, but knowing me, it's possible.

Training in Theory and Practice may have officially ended when I became a staff nurse, but my education continued. One of the many lessons I was to learn had less to do with how to practice nursing, and more with how to act like a professional nurse. This important instruction came from our unit's secretary, a kind woman around my mother's age. Several of my fellow nurses and I had been talking near enough to her desk for her to overhear me respond, "Oh God!" to something that was said. She called me aside and gently pointed out that it was quite unacceptable for me to speak like that in my position. I took her advice to heart and remained careful about my speech throughout my career, always grateful that she had taken the time to correct me.

In early spring of 1949, the position of head nurse opened up on my unit, so I applied for it. I wasn't the only one who thought she wanted the managerial position; another nurse, a year or two ahead of me also applied. I was happy to learn that I had been chosen. I felt that my superiors recognized the quality of my work and my potential for advancement. I was now the head nurse on the Medical/Surgical floor in the Memorial Unit of Concord Hospital.

Between 1950 and 1951, construction workers began transforming the maternity unit in Margaret Pillsbury's Annex II into a medical/surgical unit. Pillsbury's maternity facilities would be moved over to Memorial, and integrated into its own. But the changes didn't end there. My unit in Memorial would move into that newly renovated space on Pillsbury's Annex II.

It was disconcerting to realize that I would no longer be able to call Memorial Hospital my home, but as the construction progressed, I became excited at the prospect of being the first head nurse to manage a brand new medical/surgical unit. I could start fresh, have a sense of ownership. I would make the Margaret Pillsbury Unit of Concord Hospital my new home.

CHAPTER NINE
A HARD LESSON LEARNED

Before becoming a head nurse, the only familiarity I'd had with some of the duties of that position came from filling in when my head nurse left the unit for a few hours, or had a day off. I didn't have to make major decisions or changes, and I didn't have to carry her burden of responsibility. In fact, it wasn't much different from when I was a girl on Craney Hill, pretending I was a nurse.

But now that I was a full-time head nurse, in charge of my own unit, it became clear that I wasn't prepared for all of the duties and responsibilities that came with the position. In fact, I had no real sense of what many of them were. And I didn't have anyone checking up on me, advising me about what I should do, or not do.

In the managerial chain of command on a nursing unit, the head nurse was directly in charge of her staff. Above her was the nursing supervisor, who answered to the director. Under the best of circumstances, my nursing supervisor would have been available to counsel and critique me, but in these early days of my tenure, I went about my duties, or what I thought were my duties, with no guidance. I don't remember a time when she encouraged or even criticized me. If I approached her with a concern, I left feeling as if I had not been heard. Since neither she, nor anyone else told me otherwise, I did what I thought was best. I did what I wanted to do.

If managerial duties can be listed in order of importance with "A" being essential, "B" less important, and "C" of little importance, more often than not, I was doing "C's," when I should have been doing "A's." Finding sheets of "good paper" in the waste baskets, I retrieved them, tore them up into smaller pieces, and saved them for some yet unknown purpose. If I discovered crumbs in the bread box in my unit's kitchen, I cleaned them out when I should have been accompanying an attending physician on patient rounds. Instead, one of the nurses on my staff, realizing that I was not going, went in my place. That was not her responsibility.

My staff included two RN's from Concord Hospital, around twenty-two, my age, and two new graduates from different schools. These young women were my peers. I did not feel comfortable being their boss. Did I really want to be different from them? Not only did I want them to see me as an equal, I wanted them to like me. As a result, I wasn't critical of them. I just let them be. I went along in this manner until the day I came on shift and was summoned to a meeting by the director of nursing. I had no idea why she wanted to see me. I remember feeling apprehensive, as I left Annex II and made my way to her office in the original Margaret Pillsbury Building.

I sat opposite the buxom, straight-laced director, stiff as a board in her full white uniform and white cap. I listened in silence, tears running down my face, while she informed me that one of my nurses, speaking for my staff, had come to her to report that I had not been fulfilling my duties as head nurse.

51

The director never accused me of wrong-doing. Instead, her voice mixed with concern and compassion, she pointed out the unnecessary tasks I had spent my time on. It was painful to hear my staff's criticism, and equally upsetting to realize how much they had been floundering without proper guidance and supervision. She went on to generalize about the duties of my position, respectfully giving enough information for me to figure out the rest for myself. All I could say, when she finished speaking, was, "I'll never make a head nurse." "Yes, you will! And you'll make a good one."

The meeting was over. I dried my tears and left. The walk back to Annex II gave me time to think, and I began to feel an inner strength I hadn't felt before. I remember saying to myself, *I will prove you right. I will not let you down!* Knowing that I had the director's encouragement and support, I would use what I had heard to become the manager she knew I could be, and the boss my staff expected and needed me to be.

By the time I went through the corridor and up the stairs to my unit, I had made a decision. Right then and there, I knew that I would change myself, and when I did, a whole lot of change would happen around me. I was quiet and serious when I returned. My staff knew that I had been to the director's office, and I wanted them to see from my demeanor that I had taken her words to heart. I was ready to be the boss they deserved.

Today, I can honestly say that I am grateful to the young nurse who had the wisdom and courage to ignore the chain of command and report me to the director. I had to get called on the carpet before I was able to see what I needed to do to become a good head nurse.

The first change I made was to accompany doctors on their rounds, updating them on patients' needs and progress. Listening closely to what patients said during the visits, I got clues about what I might need to follow up on. If there were any complaints or concerns, I documented them on the scraps of paper I had taken out of waste baskets, and attached to the clipboard I always carried with me. I hadn't saved them for nothing, after all.

I made it a point to pay a daily visit on my own to each patient on my medical/surgical unit. If one of my nurses was administering hands-on care at the time, I observed her and mentored her, if necessary. If my visit took place after she had been with the patient, I checked to see that she had done her job well. I also inspected patients' beds and equipment to make certain that everything was working properly. Aside from mechanical problems, a malfunction could occur, if the attending nurse wasn't familiar with correct operation or maintenance. If that was the cause, I would gather all of my nurses and instruct them on proper use and up-keep. After a few of these conferences, I learned something about myself I hadn't known before. I liked to teach.

The instruction and guidance I gave my staff helped them to gain proficiency in their profession and feel good about themselves. But I listened and learned from them too. I encouraged suggestions for how to improve care and procedures on the unit, and when feasible, implemented them. They knew they were part of a team and that their contribution was valuable. If I was liked, it was a bonus. But it was never a goal again.

CHAPTER TEN
IT'S ABOUT TIME

When my father told me to do something on the farm, he expected it to be done well, and in a timely manner. There was no such thing as wasting time, an awareness that stayed with me when I entered training. From the beginning of my student days, I'd had a problem with the misuse of nurses' time, but it wasn't until I became head nurse that I could do something about it.

One of the most obvious places to begin was with the long accepted protocol the meds nurse followed to verify patient information before she dispensed medications to all of the patients on her unit receiving them. That information, kept at the head nurse's desk, was recorded in the Kardex, a flip-notebook with patients' names, room numbers, prescribed drug/s, dosages, and times given. To verify the Kardex information, she matched it with the same information recorded on separate, 2x2 inch Medicine Dispensing Cards, usually kept in a stack in the meds room.

All meds were dispensed on the hour, but not all patients were on the same schedule, so her first task, when she went on duty, was to find cards for all the meds due for each hour of her shift; however, there was no efficient way for her to differentiate individual patients' schedules. To save time and simplify the process, since the cards were all the same color and size, I came up with the plan to use multi-colored, 2x2 inch Medicine Dispensing Cards. Each possible schedule would be designated by its own color. If a patient was to receive medication 4x/day, beginning at 9:00 a.m., that patient's information would be recorded on a blue card. During the course of her shift, all the meds nurse had to do was reach for the stack of blue cards to match the information listed in the Kardex for patients on that schedule.

At first, the powers-that-be said I could not use this new, simplified method because other head nurses were still using the old one. But I persevered and the 2x2 inch, multi-colored Medicine Dispensing Cards became the norm on all units.

One of the most frustrating wastes of time I remembered from my days as a staff nurse occurred if a doctor, administering to a patient in his or her room, reached for a piece of equipment on a procedure tray, perhaps adhesive tape to secure an IV needle, only to find it missing. To make sure that the nurses under my supervision did not have to experience the same embarrassment, I assigned someone to stock all procedure trays, on a daily basis. From then on, everything that was supposed to be on each tray was there, and equally important, nothing was on it that didn't belong.

When my fellow head nurses and I made out our schedules, or did any paperwork for that matter, we worked at our desks, but that doesn't mean we had offices. They were out in the open, which meant we were subject to countless interruptions. Creating a schedule was one of our most important and personally time consuming duties, so to maintain the concentration needed, some head nurses created theirs away from the hospital, on their own time.

I was dedicated to my work and gave it my best effort during my scheduled hours, but I was unwilling to give up my personal time to do paperwork. How to make out my schedule, undisturbed, on hospital time? I left my unit and went back to my room in the nurses' residence. I managed to get away with it, until I got caught by the director. I can still see myself walking down the residence stairs, on my way back to the hospital, as she was walking up! Neither of us expected to see the other. Of course, the first thing she said was, "Why are you here? You should be on your floor!" She informed me that I was not to work in my room anymore. I didn't. Instead, I set up a make-shift office on my unit, in the closet used to store IV bottles and equipment. The space was too small for a chair and a desk, so I spread out my papers on a shelf and worked standing up!

As my tenure progressed, I created a Ward Manual for my staff to ensure consistency in patient care, providing information and addressing procedural questions that might arise in my absence from the floor. I wanted the nurses I supervised to be in a better position than I had been when I was a staff nurse covering for my head nurse. The manual also came in handy while I worked on scheduling, in my make-shift office. But if the nurse I assigned to manage the unit still had a question after consulting it, she knew where to find me. I was delegating responsibility and mentoring staff, while I attempted to make the best use of their time and mine.

Nurses on day shift, including head nurses, worked a staggered schedule, from 7:00 a.m.-3:30 p.m. Those who worked the split shift started at 7:00 a.m. and took a break at noon; they returned to their floor at 3:30 p.m., and worked until 7:00 p.m. The unfortunate result of the staggered shift was that nurses who were scheduled to go off duty at 3:30 p.m. would have to wait until their coworkers returned from their break to hand over patient care. Since nurses were salaried and received no over-time compensation, they waited without pay, which caused dissatisfaction and contributed to lowered staff morale.

Eventually, I was able to change this problematic scheduling for nurses working the split shift on my unit. They could finish at 11:30 a.m., rather than at noon, and return from break at 3:00 p.m., rather than 3:30 p.m. This simple time change meant that staff going off-duty could leave on time. The resulting increase in morale did not go unnoticed, and these new hours became hospital policy, until 1956, when split hours were finally discontinued.

I made one other change on my unit regarding the hand-over of patient care. It was customary for nurses on all units to stand in the linen closet during each change of shift. I felt that nurses coming off duty should be able to sit down to give their report, after having been on their feet all night. The linen closet was too small for chairs, so I placed them in an open space I'd found at the top of the stairs. Unfortunately, this change could not become hospital policy, because not all units had the luxury of an empty, open area.

The final responsibility for staff working nights was to administer a.m. patient care before their shift ended. Following standard procedure, an aide assigned to that duty would go to the utility room, fill a pitcher with water, take it to the patient's room, fill a basin for the patient to freshen up with his/her washcloth, take the basin to the utility room, empty it and return it to the patient's room. But if the unit's patient count was high, all of this going back and forth took time. One morning, I discovered that I wasn't the only one concerned with making things easier for staff, simplifying procedure, and saving time. A quick thinking aide got the pitcher of water, skipped the basins, dipped each washcloth in the pitcher, handed it to the patient, and left! Hands and faces had been washed!

And how can I forget the first year student assigned to clean the dentures of all of the patients in the seven-bed, men's ward who wore them? Apparently, her instructor had not taught her how to go about her assignment, so she came up with what she thought was a time-saving plan. Holding a basin, she went from bed to bed, asked each of the men to put his dentures inside, and carried them to the utility room to wash them. It wasn't until she returned to the ward that she realized she had no way of knowing which dentures belonged to which patient! Now what? Pass the basin around again. Good for her!

I remember all too well what it was like to be a first-year student getting an assignment, and making an attempt to get it right. Remember those scrambled eggs? I had learned that I could laugh at myself, if I did something that made me look foolish. But when I was head nurse, an incident, so embarrassing I couldn't possibly laugh, occurred on one of my daily inspection rounds. I just wanted the floor to open up beneath me.

To prevent the possibility of a spark from the electrical call bell igniting the oxygen during oxygen therapy, patients were given manual tap bells to summon help. On rounds one day, I was checking on a heart attack patient who had just completed the therapy and saw that his oxygen tent had been taken away, but the tap bell remained on his bedside table. I also observed, after talking with him, that he seemed a bit depressed. Hoping to cheer him up, I sat down next to his bed, and jokingly said as I began tapping the bell, "Let's see how long it takes for my staff to respond." We waited and waited, but not one member of my staff came in to see what was happening.

The director of nursing had also been making her rounds—the same director who had caught me on the residence stairs with my paperwork.—and this time she caught me sitting, slightly sprawled in a straight back chair, next to a patient's bed, tapping a tap bell! I immediately sat up straight and explained. I don't remember if she said anything, before she turned around and left the room. She didn't have to. Her face said it all.

All that time, the patient had been looking on, obviously enjoying my predicament, and by the time I left him, he no longer seemed depressed. Needless to say, I returned to the nurses' station and spoke to my staff about their failure to respond to what could very well have been a patient's call for assistance. It also goes without saying that I never tapped a tap bell again.

CHAPTER ELEVEN
MAKING CHANGES

My commitment to a high standard of patient care on my unit meant that I expected a great deal from my staff, but I also had the responsibility of modeling those standards to the best of my ability. From my actions, staff knew I could be trusted to treat them fairly and that I regarded them not only as professionals, but as people with personal lives and family commitments.

I felt it was important to set a congenial tone on the unit, making it possible for my staff to feel good about coming to work. It was also important that visitors felt comfortable. In the chart room, before we went on rounds and were all business, I engaged in light conversation with attending physicians, providing an opportunity to interact on a personal level. Dr. Shields, in particular, enjoyed this time and looked forward to it, once he discovered that we were both hunters—he was a bird dog hunter; I hunted for deer. When I informed him that I had shot a 175 lb, 8-point buck, on the run, he was delighted to hear that I had gotten it with one shot. From that day forward, thanks to him, I had a new nickname, "One Shot Morse!"

From the moment Dr. Shields first learned about my engagement to Malcolm, he greeted me every Monday morning with the same question, "Well, Miss Morse, did you get married this weekend? Invariably, I answered, "No." Well, you can imagine his surprise on Monday, January 4, 1954, when he asked, and I answered, "Yes, I did! Malcolm and I eloped over the weekend."

I had made the decision not to tell my staff that I had gotten married when I went into work that morning. I wanted to see if anyone would notice that I was wearing a wedding ring, so I just went about my business and waited. But as soon as Dr. Shields found out, he wanted to share the news. Without telling me what he was about to do, he left my unit and went directly to the switchboard operator, requesting that she announce my marriage over the loud speaker.

When the operator told this ex-navy man that she could do no such thing, she was told to hand over the microphone. "Now hear this! Now hear this! Miss Morse got married this weekend!" could be heard throughout the hospital! The nurses on my unit had been quietly administering morning baths, but when they heard the doctor's voice booming over the intercom, they came flying out of every room to gather around me. "Why didn't you tell us?" I replied, "Well, if you didn't notice the ring…."

If I meet any of these women today, and we get to talking about our early days, one of them is sure to remind me of that moment and tell the story to anyone who hadn't been there.

Fulfilling my commitment to having a well-run unit meant that I had plenty of opportunities to challenge the status quo and initiate policy changes. Occasionally, such an opportunity would arise from a crisis, whether as the result of an absence of established policy, or a breakdown in existing policy. No matter the cause, it required a response that would not only address the present situation, but prevent it from happening again. I can easily recall examples for both categories, each involving a surgical patient. The first crisis resulted from the lack of a set schedule for taking patients' blood pressure, including the crucial twenty-four hour period after surgery.

I had just finished listening to the night nurse's change of shift report, in which she noted that nothing of significance had occurred, and was about to begin my own morning rounds when a surgeon whose habit it was to begin his rounds very early came onto the unit. He had performed a prostatectomy on a patient of his the day before, without incident, and had come to check on him. I accompanied the doctor to the patient's room, and as soon as we entered, we realized that he was not doing well.

We immediately began looking for causes, and noticed first that there was very little fluid in the patient's urinary collection bottle. When the doctor examined the patient, he discovered that his drainage catheter, inserted during the operation, had become obstructed by a blood clot, preventing drainage. As a result, the man's bladder was full of blood. It's no overstatement to say, "All hell broke loose!" when the doctor realized what was wrong. The only recourse was for him to immediately irrigate. I assisted.

When the emergency was over, and I had time to assess what had happened, it became clear that the man had begun bleeding during the night, but simple observation by the night nurse, in all probability a student, working alone, was not enough to alert her. If she had been required to take the man's blood pressure at scheduled intervals, during the course of her shift, based on the change in readings over time, the lowered numbers would have prompted her to look for clues, discover the bleeding and alert her superior. Perhaps a more experienced nurse might have taken the patient's blood pressure as a matter of course, even though there were no orders for it on his chart, but I had no guarantees that would have happened.

I knew I couldn't do anything to change the outcome of the night before, but I could make a decision about what would happen from that morning on. Staff on my unit would take blood pressure readings every four hours, during the twenty-four hour period after surgery, day or night, even if a patient's doctor had not ordered it.

The second crisis resulted from a breakdown in an existing policy. Results of blood and urine tests, vital indicators of a patient's fitness for surgery, were posted in a patient's chart. Nurses were not expected to read or interpret them, but they were expected to make certain they had been posted. Before a scheduled surgery, the anesthesiologist would come onto the unit to check on the patient and verify the pre-op information.

One morning, the anesthesiologist and the attending nurse were in the corridor of my unit, on their way to the OR with a patient. I joined them just as the doctor was checking the man's chart. I can still see him looking for the pre-op test results, and hear him telling me they were missing. Since he couldn't find them and had no way of knowing if they had even been done, he would have to cancel the surgery. His unavoidable decision had consequences that reached beyond the patient's confusion. It would have an impact on the surgical staff, awaiting his arrival, and on the OR staff in charge of scheduling.

My first reaction was anger. *I can't believe this is happening!* And I was disappointed that the attending nurse had not done her job. But I was ultimately responsible for what happened on my unit, and I wondered where I had failed. I could not change what had happened, but I was going to make sure that this lack of documentation and accountability would not happen again.

After much thought, I created a Pre-Op Checklist, a separate sheet listing the prescribed tests for urine analysis and blood work, which would be stamped with the patient's name and location, and attached to the patient's chart. To avoid confusion, I designed it so that its size would differ from the other pages in the chart. I also suggested printing it on white paper to further distinguish it from the yellow Lab Sheet containing the test results. The attending nurse

61

would be required to look at the Lab Sheet in the patient's chart, see what tests had been done, then check them off on the checklist. Her final step in the verification process was to sign her name. That signature made her accountable.

The director of nursing approved my design for the Pre-Op Checklist, and the hospital printed and distributed it for use on all units. With minor modifications to accommodate the passage of time, the checklist is still used today.

CHAPTER TWELVE
TIME FOR SOMETHING NEW

As head nurse, I was a mentor to the young women assigned to my unit, a role I took seriously. But as my tenure progressed, I became increasingly concerned about the poor quality of students I was getting. I mentioned my concern to my friend and colleague, Georgina, who had become an instructor for first year students. She didn't agree or disagree with me. She just listened.

Years later, when we were reminiscing about our nursing careers, the subject of students came up, and Georgina finally explained why she had been silent—the nursing school's director had been sending me students who were less proficient in their clinical skills, because both she and Georgina knew that I would give these young women the extra attention they needed to succeed. Her explanation felt like a back-handed compliment when I first heard it, but I finally understood what had been going on.

After five years as head nurse, I felt I had accomplished the goals I had set for myself and my staff. Coincidentally, around that time, I was offered the position of assistant nursing instructor. Almost immediately after accepting it, however, I began having second thoughts, in spite of the fact that I had welcomed the opportunity for advancement and the new challenges the position would offer. I realized I had to tell my superior that I had changed my mind. We had a new director, and I could not be certain how she would respond. It was too late in the day to make the call, so early the next morning, I informed her that I had decided to stay where I was. Her reply, "It's too late; I've already filled your position!" My reply to her? "Well, it didn't take you long to find someone to replace me!"

Fortunately, I had no choice but to accept the position, and in September of 1955, I began to teach the basics of hands-on nursing care to first year students. My responsibilities included observing and supervising them as they practiced their skills on the medical/surgical wards of the Margaret Pillsbury Unit, which had become the site for nursing education, after the initial merger with Memorial.

One of the basic skills a nurse learns is how to administer an injection. During my own first year of training, my classmates and I learned by injecting saline solution into oranges. After we had practiced enough to satisfy the instructor, we were expected to go right out and inject patients. My first real-life experience was to give Penicillin shots to babies and small children, every three hours. The fact that I was helping them to get better gave me no comfort when I heard their cries, after pinching each little buttocks and stabbing it with the needle.

The first-year students I instructed still learned how to give shots by injecting saline into oranges, but in the few years between my student days and theirs, the hospital had instituted a new policy that required them to inject one another with a single shot of saline in class, before they injected patients. As their instructor, I could not allow them to leave until I was satisfied that they had done it correctly.

One young woman had no trouble giving an orange an injection, but the idea of sticking a needle into a person was another matter. She just couldn't do it. After the rest of her classmates had left the classroom, I told her to practice on me, and that she could not leave until she'd done so. I had no doubt that this student would be successful, but she had to find that out for herself. In spite of her apprehension, she gave me the injection. To help her feel even more confident, I encouraged her to give me a second shot. Her smile was proof that she knew she had done well.

All these years later, no matter how many times we come across one another, she reminds me of that day, and tells me that without my confidence in her, she might not have become a nurse.

In my new, instructor's role, I was able to use the experience I had gained as head nurse. Listening and observing, as I made my rounds, I got a sense of how well my students were practicing their skills, applying what they were learning in the classroom to their actual, hands-on experience. It was on one of those rounds that I went to observe a student assigned by her head nurse to bathe a patient located on Margaret Pillsbury's four-bed, men's ward, a converted sun porch with doors that opened directly to the outside.

I entered the ward and immediately realized that the young woman had been concentrating so hard on correctly administering her patient's bed bath, she was completely unaware of the fact that the head of his bed was pressing against the hot bulb of the goose-neck floor lamp, and his sheet and mattress were smoldering.

Without a word, I lifted the patient's wash basin and dumped out the bath-water, soaking the mattress, the patient, and the floor. I'll never forget the look on my student's face as she stood there, her mouth hanging open, unable to speak or to move. I ordered her to get a stretcher. We needed to get that patient out of the bed and into the hall! By then, other staff had heard the commotion and had come running. I opened the doors to the outside, and with their help, threw the mattress onto the ground. The fire department took care of it when they arrived.

I don't recall who did what next, but I know I was giving orders to get another mattress and fresh linen, make the bed, and settle the patient, by now in a fresh hospital gown, into his original place in the room. The other patients on the ward had been silently watching the whole performance, and must have been concerned, but we didn't explain or reassure. It wasn't the way. We just went back to work.

Aside from instructing and observing my students as they worked on the wards, I supervised them while they prepared meds in their assigned unit's meds room. During one of my shifts, I was helping a student who was having trouble finding a drug she needed for one of her patients. Reading the labels on the bottles, as we searched, I saw by the dates that many bottles contained meds belonging to patients who had already gone home.

Drugs prescribed to patients and charged to their accounts were referred to as special-charge drugs. Having been a head nurse, I knew that it was only after the patients had been discharged, and the head nurse on their unit returned the drugs to the pharmacy, that their accounts could be credited. For that reason, it was important that they be returned without delay. The bottles I found should not have been on those shelves, because the dates on the labels were well past the patients' discharge dates. I felt that by not following protocol, the head nurse in charge of that unit was cheating her patients. The more I thought about what I had found, the more I realized that my conscience wouldn't let me ignore it. But acting on it meant reporting her to the nursing director.

It was a ticklish situation. As an instructor, I was in a different department in the hospital. Professionally, it wasn't my place to be in this head nurse's business. Personally, and perhaps more importantly, I liked her. She was the person who had taught me to make scrambled eggs. She was my elder. I felt that if I reported her, I would be disloyal. Then there was the consideration of how the nursing director might receive the information, knowing that she had the final responsibility for what happened on her units. These findings could reflect poorly on her.

I thought a great deal about what I should do. Finally, I decided that as difficult as it might be to speak up, I couldn't keep my discovery of the special charge drugs to myself. It may have been difficult for the director to hear what I had to say, but she did listen and accept it. She could simply have pretended that she was interested, and then not done anything about it; instead she ended the meeting by telling me that she would pass my report along to the hospital administrator. When I left her office, I was relieved. I had no idea what would happen. I only knew that I had done what I had to do.

A few days later, the director filled me in about what had transpired during her meeting with the administrator. He was in the process of re-evaluating the duties and requirements for the day supervisor of nursing's position, and was looking for someone capable of taking on more responsibility and acting, in effect, as an assistant director. After hearing my report on the special charge drugs, he told the director, "She's just the gal we need!"

The next thing I knew, I was being offered the position. I would be replacing the nurse who had been my supervisor when I was head nurse. I had promised myself back then, that one day I would have her job, and when I did, unlike her, I would provide the head nurses I supervised with the guidance they needed. I would listen and help them to rely on their own strength, but they would never have to feel that they were alone.

I was aware that this newly defined, supervisory position would not be without its challenges. The first to come to mind was the fact that as a student, I had worked under the supervision of all of the head nurses who would now answer to me. But I knew I was ready. And I didn't even have to apply for the job.

CHAPTER THIRTEEN
NEW TITLE, NEW HOSPITAL

I stepped into the position of day supervisor of nursing services comfortable in the knowledge that I had the full support of the director of nursing, as I assumed the higher level of responsibility it required. If I saw that changes in policies or procedure needed to be made, I would have the freedom and the clout necessary to make them. That was right up my alley. My title might be different, but my on-going commitment to raising the standard of nursing care, while maintaining an atmosphere of respect for staff and patients, would remain the same.

I continued the routines I had set in place as head nurse, visiting patients and asking if they had any concerns about their care. I checked their medical equipment and instructed nurses on proper use and maintenance. Before morning rounds, I received the night supervisor's verbal report on the conditions of patients on all medical/surgical units, addressing concerns or problems, including any with staff. I never asked my care-givers to perform a task that I was not willing to perform, even in a non-nursing situation. If mealtime was half an hour, I didn't take a minute longer.

As I familiarized myself with how the head nurses under my supervision ran their units, I paid special attention to how they scheduled their staff's work, vacation, and break times, while maintaining sufficient patient coverage. Reviewing their time books to get a sense of their daily schedules, I saw that each head nurse made out her schedule only one week in advance. This practice concerned me, because it made it possible for a head nurse to get away with favoring certain staff members with holidays and week-ends off. Further investigation revealed that was the case on some of the units.

When I was head nurse, I had made out my schedule to cover a four-week period, which allowed me to plan for sufficient coverage and attend to the needs of my staff. They were able to know when they worked and had time off well enough in advance to make plans in their personal lives. Equally important, they saw that no one received preferential treatment, which had the potential to contribute to poor morale.

Having experienced the value of a four-week schedule, I made its implementation mandatory for the head nurses I supervised. I also restructured and standardized their daily assignment sheets to include staff meal and break times, along with any assigned non-nursing duties. Each morning, when I came on duty, I compared the daily time sheets with the patient census reports, and if necessary, temporarily reassigned staff to make certain that all units were adequately covered. I can recall only one time when a nurse I had reassigned to an under-staffed floor protested the change. I told her she could either go to work, where she was most needed, or take her next holiday time off. She chose the holiday. Her decision was fine with me, and her head nurse had no objection. By now, I had learned my lesson. I did my job. Never mind who got mad.

In May of 1956, the Margaret Pillsbury Unit and the Memorial Unit of Concord Hospital physically merged in their new, permanent location on Pleasant Street in Concord, NH. I looked forward to continuing my commitment to providing a balanced and humane work environment in our new home. The four-winged, Concord Hospital had five floors; the fifth floor served as quarters for nursing students. Its three medical/surgical units were equipped with twenty beds on each, including those in private and semi-private rooms. All of the beds were new and could be easily raised and lowered, a welcome help for nurses. Now, when a patient signaled for assistance, a light came on above the bed, above the door outside the room, and at the nurses' station. (Tap bells were still given to patients during oxygen therapy).

For the first time in our history, patients' rooms had sinks in them. No more getting water from the utility room. And no more communal bed pans and urinals; patients had their own. In fact, the two private rooms on each unit shared a toilet. Each unit also had a two-stall bathroom, with a sink and toilet designated for male and female ambulatory patients. Nursing staff still cleaned bed pans, urinals, and everything else they were responsible for in the old hospital, until the housekeeping department came into being.

In time, a transportation department was created to escort new patients from admitting to their assigned units, or to X-Ray, relieving nurses of a duty that had taken them away from hands-on patient care. Central Sterile Supply, supervised by an RN, took over the OR staff's responsibility for sterilizing surgical instruments and medical equipment.

Meal service for patients underwent changes as well. Head nurses no longer served food from steam carts. The main kitchen delivered individual trays of food, prepared according to patients' needs, desert included. Nursing staff still distributed the meals, picking them up from the portable cart. When meals were finished, they collected the trays and returned them to the cart. Main kitchen staff returned them to the kitchen, freeing nurses to assist patients who could not feed themselves, or needed help. The changes also meant the elimination of the civilian kitchen aide's position and a familiar presence in our units' kitchens.

I'll never forget walking past the open kitchen door on my unit, in the old hospital, in time to catch the civilian aide, her apron over her street clothes, stooping down to pick up a serving of Jell-O she had dropped on the floor. With her bare hands, she placed it back in its dish, and put the dish on a patient's tray. When I told her that she could not serve that Jell-O and had to go back to the main kitchen and get another serving, she became upset, but not because she'd been caught doing something unsanitary. She didn't want to have to explain why she needed a replacement.

I settled into the new Concord Hospital, acquainting myself with its new equipment, departments, and policies. As I made my rounds on the new units, I was more aware of some of the policies and procedures from the old hospital that had remained. For example, staff still carried the wire racks containing the thermometers, in their glass tubes, to the patient's bedside. As before, the tubes were labeled with patient identification, but on more than one occasion, I witnessed patients having their temps taken with someone else's thermometer.

Determined to rectify this intolerable situation, I proposed we do away with the carry-rack, and permanently attach a metal holder to the bedpost at the head of each patient's bed. The nurse would place the glass tube containing the thermometer inside, eliminating any chance of a mix-up. The hospital administration accepted my suggestion, and the men in the hospital's Maintenance Department implemented it. I even received $5.00 when my idea was written up in the *Journal of Nursing.*

Occasionally, on my rounds, it was necessary to step in to assist staff, or to intervene in a crisis. One such intervention occurred as I entered a women's ward, and from my vantage point, was able to observe that the arm of a patient receiving an IV treatment was twice its normal size. The attending student nurse was standing near the bed, engaged in a conversation with her nursing instructor, and neither of them was aware that the IV fluid had been running into the woman's soft tissue, rather than into her vein.

I immediately stopped the IV and told the instructor to call the unit's head nurse to come and re-start it. By the1950's, nurses in our hospital had been given the power to start IV's. I can't say for certain how the change in policy came about; it could have been a way for doctors to save time. Whatever the reason, we had made some progress.

When I think about that woman lying in that bed, silently watching her arm blow up like a balloon, I can't help but wonder whether a male patient in the same predicament would have spoken out, and gotten his nurse's attention.

Not all of my interventions resulted from an emergency situation. If I observed that a protocol had not been followed, I stepped in. Such was the case the morning I looked in on a patient placed on precaution and noticed that her food tray was still in her room. Staff entered the rooms of patients on precaution only when necessary, to minimize the possibility of contamination. It was well past breakfast, and I was concerned that both the tray and the patient had been forgotten, and she might be feeling neglected.

I visited with the woman for a while, and when I left her room, I went looking for the unit's head nurse to tell her to have the tray removed. It was the same nurse who had not reported the special charge drugs when I was an instructor. I genuinely liked her, but once again I found myself in the uncomfortable position of pointing out something she had not done. She didn't say anything in response. The tray was removed, and that was the end of it.

My perception now, as I recall this encounter, is that I was offering a staff member the guidance I would have appreciated from my supervisor when I was a head nurse. I can't say that my perception was shared, but I do believe that my staff knew that I was continually evaluating their work and their working environment, so that we could all meet a high standard of nursing care. They might not have liked what I required of them at times, but I think I can say with some certainty that they did respect it.

CHAPTER FOURTEEN
FAMILY? CAREER?

My rounds were interrupted one morning by an announcement to report to the director's office. When I got there, I discovered that my co-worker, Louise, had also been summoned. Neither of us knew why. We were surprised to learn that the director would be leaving Concord Hospital and embarking on an adventure in a totally new environment. It was 1960, the hospital ship operated by Project Hope was making its maiden voyage to Indonesia, and she was going to be its director of nursing! Louise and I were excited for her, and after expressing our best wishes, we took the opportunity to make announcements of our own.

I was going to have my first child and would be taking maternity leave. Louise revealed that she was pregnant and would also be leaving. It was going to be a mass exit, and we were learning about it at the same time. I can still see the three of us sitting in that office, sharing our plans and dreams. I had been concerned about how I was going to break the news of my departure and felt relieved that I was able to, under such happy circumstances.

Not long after, I was offered the director's position, but I knew my limits by this time, and declined. However, I gladly assumed the role of acting director for two months and was privileged to orient the new director of nursing when she arrived. Before I left on maternity leave, the whole hospital, including the boiler men, surprised me with a baby shower. My son, Tim, was born on November 3, 1960.

When my leave was over, I realized I wanted to stay at home and be a full-time mom, so in January of 1961, after having been the assistant director of nursing for five years, I resigned. My resignation was accepted with regret, and the anticipation of my return in the future. The decision to leave had not been an easy one. I knew I would miss all of the people who made up the community of Concord Hospital, an important part of my life for twelve years. I also wondered what would happen to the standards and policies I had put in place, fought for in some cases, during my time there.

Tim was about a year and a half when I got a call from the nursing director at the hospital. They would appreciate my return on a call-in basis, if I were interested. I was. I had discovered that as much as I enjoyed spending time with my son, dirty floors and dirty dishes didn't interest me all that much. I was happy for the opportunity to run away. Truthfully, it was more like running back to feeling the way I had when I was Bertha McComish, Assistant Administrative

Nursing Supervisor, using the nursing knowledge and experience I had worked hard to attain, and making a difference in peoples' lives.

I was well aware that when I returned to the hospital, my responsibilities as wife and mother would not simply disappear, and that I was expected to make the adjustments necessary in order to carry them out. As a call-in, I might be asked to go in for the day shift, from 7:00 a.m.-3:30 p.m., or at night, from 3:00 p.m.-11:30 p.m. Either way, I needed someone to look after Tim. Malcolm was working the farm, and since hiring a babysitter was not yet a common practice, I would have to rely on my mother and sister, and Malcolm's mother to look after my son.

It took work to go back to work. No matter who looked after Tim, I still had to pack everything he would need and then load all of that, and him, into the car. It was a challenge just to get out of the house, especially on the days everything seemed to go wrong; the days I wished I had help. I was always in a hurry! I can't forget the time I scratched the stainless steel kitchen cabinet with the metal frame of Tim's folding playpen, rushing to get out the door.

I also can't forget having to stand up to my mother-in-law when she questioned my decision to allow my neighbors to look after Tim one day. An older couple who loved him like grandparents, they had often asked if they could watch him while I was at work. I finally agreed, but the following day, as I was settling Tim in at Grammie McComish's, she completely ignored me. It was her way of letting me know how much she had disapproved of my decision to share her grandson. "Well," I told her, "if you're going to act that way, I'll take him back there today." She turned around and faced me. After that, our neighbors watched Tim when it was convenient, and Grammie McComish never said a word. I knew I had to make the choice to confront, not just for my sake, but for Tim's and our neighbors'. I wasn't about to have my mother-in-law control my actions.

There were other challenges, as I prepared for my shift; a few sapped what little energy I had some days, but I wasn't about to let them stop me. I was back doing the work I loved, and being acknowledged and appreciated for it. And that energized me.

I continued working as a call-in, until I resigned in February of 1963, two months before the birth of my second son, Dennis. I waited until he was around a year and a half, before resuming some private duty work. Now I had two children to get ready and drop off.

In 1965, I decided I wanted to return to Concord Hospital on a call-in basis. Once again it felt good to be back. Not long after my return, the director of nursing told me that she had recommended me for a consulting position. The administrator of Franklin Hospital had contacted her, looking for someone on her staff with managerial experience. His director of nursing services had left, and the acting director was having a difficult time filling in. The position was part-time and would not interfere with my schedule at Concord Hospital, so I agreed to take it. In his letter confirming my acceptance, Franklin's administrator added that I could decide how much time I wanted to spend on-site. I also had the option to work on my plans at home. Initially, I spent my time observing how the hospital's nursing department was being run.

Since I was an outsider, I was able to identify problems and recommend solutions without fear of the political consequences. There was no question that the acting director was a good nurse, but it became clear that he lacked the administrative skills necessary to effectively push his agenda forward. He desired to be liked by his staff and was afraid of making decisions that would displease them. I knew from personal experience that unless he changed his behavior, he would not be able to make the necessary, managerial changes.

I limited my time on-site to one day a week, and did my planning and preparation at home. Working with the acting director and the nurses he supervised, I was able to evenly distribute the workload and clarify the duties of staff and supervisors. It was gratifying to know that I had the support of Franklin's administrator, as I suggested changes and helped to implement them. But, more often than not, I met with resistance from the acting director. All too often I heard, "We can't do that!" Regardless, I persevered. Like getting those heifers in their right stalls when I was eleven years old, I wasn't going to quit until I had set things right.

After two years, I realized that I had accomplished as much as I could, in spite of the pushback, a fact acknowledged by Franklin's administrator. In his letter thanking me for all of my hard work, he assured me that my "heartaches were not in vain," acknowledging that I had left "plenty of homework" for the acting director to continue in my absence. Two years later, I received another letter offering me the position of director of nursing services, on a part-time basis. I declined.

All the while I was consulting at Franklin Hospital, I had continued my call-in work at Concord Hospital, until I was very pregnant with my third child. I remember making rounds when a male patient commented that I was "a bit round." I guess I was! I resigned in October of 1968, and my daughter, Nancy, was born in November. I knew I wanted to be home with my little girl, and for the most part, I was.

Between Nancy's birth and when she turned five, I worked sporadically, mostly as a private duty nurse for Henniker residents, in their homes, or at the hospital. Mainly I spent time with Nancy and the boys. I could take all three to visit family any time I wanted to. In summer, the boys went swimming in the pond, when they weren't off riding the tractor with their dad to get water for the cows, a chore they loved. Malcolm's farm work kept him away from home as much as it always had, but I enjoyed the time I had with the children. During those years, I felt that I had the best of both worlds.

Around the time Nancy turned five, however, something changed. I felt I was not being challenged. I knew I needed to get back to being a part of the medical community at Concord Hospital, but I also was concerned that the duties of my position might have

75

changed too much in my absence. Despite my fears and concerns, and no matter how much I felt like an outsider, I knew I had to call my former boss and ask if I could come back. I was certain I did not want to resume a full-time career, so when I asked if I could come back as a call-in, she immediately replied, "Yes."

It felt good to return, but that five year absence did mean that I was required to go through re-orientation for my supervisory position. Until I could resume work on my own, I would follow the nursing supervisor for the 3:00 p.m.-11:30 p.m. shift, on her rounds. She was an older woman who had previously worked in the OR.

I noticed that when we entered a patient's room, the supervisor would ask, "How are you today?" But she always left before the patient had a chance to answer; her parting words, "Fine, Fine." trailing after her. Off she'd go to the next, and the next, "How are you, today? Good, good." Never hearing a word any of the patients said! I thought to myself, *I'm not going to do what she does.* I'm surprised I never said something to this woman. It must have taken a lot for me to keep my mouth shut. Writing about her now, I found myself wondering if her lack of listening skills was a result of her previous work in the OR, where her patients were in no position to speak.

Returning to Concord Hospital meant a return to getting help with childcare. By now, with three children, I was comfortable with the decision to hire a babysitter. I knew that it was up to me to find the right person, and pay her. I felt fortunate when I found a young girl who could come to my house. Her mother brought her before I left for work, and came to pick her up when Malcolm got back from the farm. If I worked a later shift, I prepared the evening meal for everyone, before I went. I have to admit that sometimes I felt conflicted about leaving my family to go to work. I remember how bad I felt the day Tim, my oldest, tied his wagon to the back wheel of my car. I couldn't pull out of the driveway until I untied it! But I did, and went on my way.

76

I also must admit that as happy as I was to be back at work, I was disheartened to learn that, in my absence, little had been done to eliminate, or at least reduce, the number of non-nursing duties expected of staff, and that included supervisors. The hospital continued to have only one of us on duty for each shift, so I could be called away from my own responsibilities to take on any number of time-consuming tasks, anywhere within the building. The stock room and pharmacy were located in the basement, but were only staffed during business hours, Monday through Friday. The morgue, also in the basement, was not staffed at all. As supervisor, I had the keys to all three locations.

If supplies or equipment were needed anywhere in the hospital, including the OR, after closing, and on weekends and holidays, I would have to go down to the stock room and search for the requested supplies and deliver them. If a doctor prescribed medication for a patient, after hours, I went down to the pharmacy and filled the prescription, with the exception of narcotics. Once I located the meds and bottled them, I typed up the label, a one-finger operation for me, then placed them in the dumbwaiter in the hall, and sent them up. Hearing my name called over the loud-speaker and wondering who was trying to find me added stress to an already stressful situation. Since one of my own duties as supervisor was to confer with the admitting clerk about availability of beds on the units, it might be a doctor needing a bed for an incoming patient; however, there was always the possibility that a nurse needed my assistance, and I wasn't there for her.

When one of our patients died, I accompanied the nurse responsible for delivering the deceased to the morgue. If a death occurred outside the hospital, in the case of an accident, or under unusual circumstances, the body would be transported to our morgue for examination by the coroner. He did not have an office on the premises, so when he arrived, I would be called to escort him to the morgue and remain with him, until he determined cause of death and signed the death certificate.

Eventually, a security officer accompanied the nurse and escorted the coroner to the morgue, but supervisors were still expected to fill prescriptions and get supplies. The day came, however, when I could no longer continue to be called away to attend to disruptive tasks, without voicing my objection. In 1977, I documented them and wrote to the director of nursing, asking they be eliminated. In her written response to my letter, she validated my observation:

***

This is the type of information we need to get some action.
Though I can't promise immediate results, we will get somewhere
if we continue to hang in. [...] I presented your
'evidence' of a supervisor doing everybody else's job....

***

The changes I advocated for did not happen overnight, but in time, many of the non-supervisory duties were eliminated, relieving me not only of the necessity of performing them, but of the burden of fighting to end them. I finally felt free to do the job I thought I was supposed to be doing—mentoring, educating, and supporting nurses.

During the span of my nursing career, I had made difficult decisions in my professional and personal lives, especially when I had to choose between responsibilities to my family and my need to fulfill myself, through my work. In spite of challenges, I forged ahead, grateful for the support and encouragement I received from my superiors.

Since I have usually said what is on my mind, to be true to myself in these pages, I feel it is necessary to reveal that in the 1970's, having struggled with circumstances in my life that were physically and emotionally exhausting, it had become obvious that I could no longer go on without support from a source beyond anything I had known. I am forever thankful for an invitation to a weekly Bible Study group during this time. Thinking I had nothing to lose, I attended. There, under the pastor's teaching from the Bible, I learned my need for salvation. Accepting Jesus Christ as my personal Lord and Savior was the beginning, and continues to be my hope and encouragement through struggles and disappointments.

Using what I had learned in my own life, professionally and personally, I shared my own experience, when it was welcome, with staff who spoke about their difficulties maintaining a balance between family and career. Most of all, I listened. They knew that someone cared, and that they were appreciated.

I would like to say that I continued my nursing career, until I retired, without ever again having to choose between career and family, but that was not the case. However, no matter when I was faced with that choice, I always chose family, even when it meant giving up my position and the seniority I had earned. Even when it meant having to leave *my hospital.*

CHAPTER FIFTEEN
A NURSE IS A NURSE…

Although professional and personal challenges for nurses remain, the role of nurse has changed dramatically since the 1940's when we asked permission to leave the unit at the end of a shift. No longer relegated to collecting soap for enemas, today's nurses have become doers in their own right, performing many of the procedures that once were solely a doctor's domain. When I was a head nurse, accompanying a doctor on rounds, he told me to put the blood pressure cuff on his patient's arm, so that he could take her blood pressure. I did it, but in my mind I was thinking, *Do it yourself.*

Nurses of my generation worked in an era when supplies and equipment were not easily attainable, and certainly not disposable. Let's not forget having to boil those rubber tubes. We were taught to be frugal. Standing beside doctors, we counted out the gauze squares and sponges we handed them. The fact that I was a head nurse, in charge of my own unit, did not save me from a reprimand for having removed too many sponges from their sterile container.

One of the most visible changes in my profession is the way nurses dress for work. Today, a visitor to Concord Hospital might have to ask a care-giver's title, since the traditional white uniform and starched, white cap have gone the way of white stockings, and white, laced shoes. (Obviously, I am referring specifically to women's uniforms, since male nurses were a rarity in the hospitals where I studied and worked, especially early in my career.)

Changes in dress began in our hospital in the 1980's when a newly hired director came to work in street clothes. It wasn't long before directors of the maternity and intensive care units were wearing street attire, neckerchiefs and bows with fancy knots. Next, nurses in the children's wards were clamoring to be allowed to wear colored tops, with white skirts or pants. My only concession at the time was to trade in my white, laced shoes for white, slip-ons, a modification that went unnoticed by visitors passing me in the corridor one day. I overheard one of them say, "There goes a real nurse."

I suspect that the length of the uniforms my classmates and I wore in the 1940's might have caused a stir for our predecessors who wore theirs down to their ankles. But I'm certain we would all agree that the way a nurse dresses has nothing to do with how well she cares for her patients.

On January 9, 1993, wearing my full, white uniform and cap, I worked as a supervisor at Concord Hospital for the last time. (By now, there were two supervisors on a shift.) Co-workers from my supervisory team organized a retirement party for me, and among the guests were doctors and nurses who had been part of my history at Concord Hospital, but were no longer working there.

I didn't know it, but in preparation for the party, my co-worker had gone around with a tape recorder, asking staff to recount their personal experiences of having worked under my supervision. One of the aides on maternity shared how when I would find her sitting at the nurses' station "doing nothing," I would make arrangements with her charge RN to assign her to a unit, where her "assistance would be appreciated." She soon learned it would be wise to disappear when she saw me arrive, but I always followed her and reassigned her. The aide concluded her story with, "She's the lady who taught me I could run, but I couldn't hide!"

A second story from that joyous and memorable evening is about an interaction between me and my supervisor. Every day, when I arrived for work on the 3:00-11:30 p.m. shift, I went into the staff room, where I would find the dirty lunch tray she had left behind when she returned to her duties. One day, I'd had enough. I got a paper towel, drew a Frown Face on it and wrote, "Take me back to the kitchen!" and placed it on her tray. Neither one of us had ever spoken about what I had done, so you can imagine how surprised I was, during the party, when my former supervisor handed me a drawing of a Frown Face on a paper towel! We shared a laugh about it.

Everyone knew that when I retired, I planned to write a book about my nursing experience, so among the gifts I received were a scrapbook for my memories, and writing materials to help me keep my promise. As it turned out, however, my dream of writing was put on hold. I had retired from my career at Concord Hospital, but my retirement from nursing was short-lived. In 1994, I began a four-year long journey of taking care of my husband, Malcolm. It was important to us that he would remain at home, after he experienced a second, in-operable bout with colon cancer.

In a hospital setting, nurses see patients during the critical time of an illness or surgery, and in the best of circumstances, during their recovery. Since we have no further contact with them when they're discharged, we don't know what they and their families must do to manage care and go on with their lives. But now, caring for Malcolm at home, I would find out. Although I was more qualified than most family members because of my training, I still felt over-loaded with the responsibility. Once again, I was in a position to learn something new about being a nurse.

As a supervisor, working eight hours a day, five days a week, I had managed the care of patients through the services of my staff, but for the first time in many years, I returned to being a hands-on nurse, working alone, twenty-four hours a day, every day.

Toward the end of the four year period, the *Concord Monitor* was planning to publish an article on Home Health Care vs. Nursing Home Care, and I received an invitation to be interviewed. I declined at first, saying I couldn't possibly take on another commitment in my already over-taxed life. However, after much thought, I reconsidered. I realized it was important for me to share what I had been learning in this new phase of care-giving.

A reporter and a photographer from the paper came to our home, and *In Good Hands*, the beautifully written, in-depth account of the joys and burdens of caring for a loved one at home was published on October 11, 1998. Among the lessons I had learned and shared were the need for self-care and the willingness to accept help when offered. It was gratifying to receive responses from people who had read the article and shared with me how helpful it had been.

I had promised Malcolm that he would not go to a nursing home. I kept my promise. Seventeen evenings after publication of the article, with his loving family around him, my husband went home to be with The Lord.

CHAPTER SIXTEEN
IN CLOSING

After Malcolm's passing, I knew that I needed to make a new life for myself, and that meant getting out, meeting new people, and doing new things. But I kept up with my former colleagues from Concord Hospital, too. I continue to attend lunches and retirement parties and remain in contact, both by letters and phone calls, with those who are no longer able to gather in person. One of my correspondents is nearly one hundred years old!

I have time to create with cloth— clothing, bags, and quilts. And I bake. My grandchildren, who range in age from seven to twenty-three, have been and are the joy of my life, and all have learned how to sew and bake from their Grammie. I've taught neighbors and friends, as well. I also take part in the activities of our local senior center.

I enjoy the beauty of the seasons, and still take my long, daily walks, when I'm able, alongside my country road, once a dirt road, where cows could be driven "up-road." An impossibility today, because of the traffic. Open fields, where I snow-shoed, have grown up to large trees. I haven't snow-shoed in a few years, and I gave up hunting fifty-four years ago. But I have, on occasion, taken a shot at a wood chuck I've caught eating my garden vegetables!

Being a retired nurse has not prevented me from staying current with what is happening today in medicine and nursing, or in sharing my knowledge. When I have the opportunity to administer hands-on care, I am happy to do so.

My original goal for writing about my nursing career was to document, from years of notes, the working and learning conditions, and the attitudes of my era. I hoped that nurses of today could know and appreciate that period in their history. In my early attempts, I would usually end up erasing, or changing the order of what I was writing. As a result, it was hard to make any progress. I found myself discouraged and overwhelmed. Realizing that I was going to need help, if I wanted to accomplish the work, was a blessing. With that help, I also realized that there was more to writing than chronicling "just the facts." I had begun journaling when I was nine years old, but I had not planned on going back to revisit that early writing, or my life on Craney Hill, until I came to understand that if I were going to write about my life as a nurse, I would have to explore the circumstances that helped me prepare for it.

I had no idea, when I started, how long it would take to write the book you now hold in your hands. Or how emotionally draining it would be to write about the experiences I had chosen to include. Sometimes I felt anger or sadness, all over again—sometimes for the first time. Like many of my fellow nurses, I had blocked them out years ago, in order to go on. Recalling the times when events had been out of my control made me wonder if I could have done more to change the outcome. Fortunately, I was also able to laugh while writing about situations that were funny! I have come to recognize that the work ethic I had been taught on the farm, and practiced in my career, has helped me to turn my desire to write my book into a reality.

Grateful is what I am, for all who have traveled with me on this journey. Thank You.

PHOTOGRAPHS

The house and barn on Craney Hill, and the oxen Bertha drove.

Bertha, left, age ten; her sister Mary, eight, is on the right. In the background is the family's Model-T Ford, and the corn shed where ears of corn were dried to be fed to the pigs and/or ground up for corn meal.

Bertha and Mary outside the cottage where their brother Forrest was born.

Bertha's walk from the stone wall at the end of her dad's corn field through the woods to Mount Hunger.

89

Leaving Craney Hill

Bertha driving the oxen pulling the playhouse

built for Mary and her by their dad.

Bertha in her summer Cadet Corps nurse's uniform.

91

…and in her winter Cadet Corps uniform.

92

Bertha in her first six months of training, 1945, outside the Memorial Hospital, Concord, New Hampshire.

93

Bertha on the steps of Bellevue Hospital, New York, New York.

Side-view of Bellevue Hospital from Bertha's residence window.

Nursing Supervisor, Bertha McComish, outside the nursing administrative office, Concord Hospital, Concord, New Hampshire, 1992.

Acknowledgments
In appreciation of all who have graciously given their time, resources,
encouragement, and suggestions during the creation of this book,

Particular thanks to

Nancy McComish, Fran Chelland, Dan Waber, Carolyn Gregsak,
Priscilla Soukas, Kimberly Nelson Hall, Fatima and Jeremy
McHugh, Mary-Catherine Jones, and Joseph Hurka.

ENDNOTES

In 1890, George Pillsbury of Minneapolis, Minnesota, a former resident and city official of Concord, New Hampshire, pledged a donation of land and a new hospital building to be built on it, in honor of his wife. The Margaret Pillsbury General Hospital was dedicated in 1891.

In 1896, the New Hampshire Memorial Hospital for Women and Children was established. Its mission was to serve New Hampshire's women and children in need who wished to be cared for by women physicians and attendants. By 1930, Memorial became the greater Concord area's second general hospital.

***

We felt at the time that in winning the war, the future held great promise. Today our nation has never stood at greater peril. If the nursing profession is to take its rightful place in future planning, it is the nurses themselves who must present a united front to further the interest of nurses, and in a larger sense, the nursing profession, by doing everything possible to elevate standards of nursing care and improving the health of our communities. It is only by action that we can fulfill our obligation.

Florence M. Clark,
President of the New Hampshire State Nurses' Society, 1944-1946
Published in 1956, in a booklet commemorating the society's 50th Anniversary.

ABOUT THE AUTHORS

BERTHA McCOMISH was born on July 9th, a rainy night in 1927, in Henniker, NH—the first baby born in the Henniker Maternity Home, alongside the Contoocook River. She grew up on a farm on Craney Hill. After high school, where she was voted "hardest working," she entered nurses' training through the United States Nurse Cadet Corps. After graduation from the Memorial Hospital Unit of Concord Hospital, Concord, NH, in 1948, she went on to become a head nurse, a nursing instructor, and a nursing supervisor. She retired from her supervisory position in 1993, and has been busy ever since. She is pleased to have had the opportunity to tell her story.

***

MAGGIE MARTIN is a published poet, writer, and educator who, for over twenty-five years, has helped people of all ages write their stories. A native of Northeastern PA, she now makes her home in Henniker, NH, not too far from her granddaughters, Abby and Sophie, who happen to be Bertha's grandchildren, as well.

Made in the USA
Charleston, SC
30 October 2014